How To Obtain Strong Faith

by

Frederick K.C. Price, D.D.

FAITH ONE
PUBLISHING
LOS ANGELES, CALIFORNIA

12th Printing

How To Obtain Strong Faith
ISBN 1-883798-70-1
Copyright © 1977 by Frederick K.C. Price, D.D.
(Revised Edition 1980)
P.O. Box 90000
Los Angeles, CA 90009

Published by Faith One Publishing
7901 South Vermont Avenue
Los Angeles, California 90044

Contents

1

Know the Reality of God's Word

Too many of us as Christians are weak. Too many
of us as Christians live on the weak level of
inadequacy. Too many of us as Christians live on the
weak plateau of defeatism because we have not risen
to that plateau of strength where God meant for us as
Christians to live. Yet the Bible encourages us to be
"strong in the Lord and in the power of His might"
(Ephesians 6:10). No one can be strong in the Lord
without being strong in faith. Therefore, I want to talk
to you through these printed pages about **"How To
Obtain Strong Faith — Six Principles."** If you understand these six fundamentals, and if you will begin to
exercise and use them, you will arrive at the place
where God can say of you, "You have strong faith."

All through the Gospels we are constantly
reminded of what Jesus often had to say to His
disciples: "Oh ye of little faith; of ye of little faith."
Over and over again Jesus had to say, "Oh ye of little
faith." (Matthew 6:30; 14:31; 16:8; Luke 12:28.)

Little faith would be weak faith, wouldn't it?
Little would represent that which is weak; weakness is
the opposite of strength and strength is the opposite of
weakness.

Now, God is strong. The Bible says that He is a
strong tower, a citadel of protection and redemption.

The Bible says that God is almighty and it encourages us to be strong *in the Lord.*

The Bible says that Abraham was not weak in faith but STRONG! The Bible tells us that **Abraham was strong in faith.**

"As it is written, I have made thee a father of many nations, before him whom he believed, even God, who quickeneth the dead, and calleth those things which be not as though they were. Who against hope believed in hope, that he might become the father of many nations, according to that which was spoken, So shall thy seed be. And being not weak in faith, he considered not his own body now dead, when he was about an hundred years old, neither yet the deadness of Sarah's womb: He staggered not at the promise of God through unbelief; but was strong in faith, giving glory to God; And being fully persuaded, that what he, (God) had promised, he was able also to perform" (Romans 4:17-21).

Faith Is The Key—

In the above Scripture, the Apostle Paul is talking about faith. He uses Abraham, one of the Old Testament patriarchs, as an illustration of faith. He points out the fact that Abraham, though an old man and well stricken in years, and Sarah his wife, being barren, did not have any children — yet God said to Abraham that at a certain time next year, they would have a child. Sarah would give birth to a child!

Now, in the natural everything was opposed to that. In the natural it was *impossible* for Abraham and Sarah to have a child. BUT GOD SAID THAT THEY WOULD HAVE A CHILD. Abraham didn't consider the circumstances; he didn't consider the fact that he was old and that Sarah was barren. The Bible says of him, "He was not weak in faith, but he was STRONG in FAITH, giving glory to God."

The reason that Abraham could be strong and give God the glory was because he was FULLY PERSUADED. It said that he was fully persuaded that what God said would happen would. God was able to do it, Abraham believed Him; and the Bible said that he was a man possessed of "STRONG FAITH."

Faith is the key that unlocks the treasure chest of heaven. Faith is the key that moves the hand of the Almighty. Faith is the key by which you can obtain the desires of your heart. Faith is that which pleases God.

We want to look at another verse of Scripture that goes along with what we have just read. Paul is speaking to the Ephesians, and of course he is speaking to all of us who are Christians who believe God's Word, all who have been born again by the Spirit of God. Paul says, "Finally, my brethren, be strong in the Lord, and in the power of his might" (Ephesians 6:10). "Be strong in the Lord." Not weak in the Lord, but "**be strong in the Lord, and in the power of his might.**" In both of these Scriptures that we have just read, we see the word "strong." In one case we find that it says that Abraham had strong faith and that his faith was commended by God.

If we are going to be faith children of a faith God, then we too must be strong. Paul tells us here, "Be strong in the Lord." Now, we cannot be strong in the Lord without having strong faith, because faith is the key that opens the treasure chest of heaven. It is faith that pleases God, and it is by faith and through faith that we obtain the promises of God.

You see, my friend, when you have strong faith you can overcome any obstacle. When you have strong faith, there are no mountains that are too high for you to cross over. When you have strong faith, there are no valleys that are too wide for you to pass through. When you have strong faith, you cannot be defeated. So, the watchword for us as Christians is to "BE STRONG IN THE LORD AND IN THE POWER OF HIS MIGHT."

Faith Comes From God—

Now remember that faith comes from God: Faith is a gift that God gives us at the new birth. He gives us faith, but that faith has to be developed. It has to be matured. That faith has to be brought to a place of strength.

When a baby is born into the world, it is not physically strong. A baby is physically weak, but if you give it enough time, if you give it enough exercise, enough rest, enough food, enough nourishment, that baby will grow from a state of weakness to a state of strength.

Like that newborn baby, each one of us as Christians, when we are born again by the Spirit of God, has imparted to us God's measure of faith, but that faith in us at that moment is weak. It is by us using that faith, understanding the principles of faith and then exercising those principles that we can arrive at strong faith. We arrive at a place where nothing will be impossible to us, where we can be the victors and masters in every circumstance. For Jesus said, "To him that believeth, **ALL** things are possible" — not some things are possible, not a few things are possible — but Jesus said, "To him that believeth, all things are possible" (Mark 9:23).

Can you dare to believe that? Can you dare to rise to that level and believe and claim that, and act on it?

Thank God! That's where I am. I didn't say that I am perfect. No! But I praise God that I want to exercise STRONG faith. I know how to do it because God's Word tells me how, and I want to share it with you.

If you are to obtain strong faith, then the first thing that it will be necessary for you to do is to learn that *God's Word is real.* You must know the reality of the Word of God; not guess about it, not philosophize about it, not hope about it, but you must KNOW THE REALITY OF GOD'S WORD.

Get God's Word Off That Page And Down Into Your Spirit—

You see, God's Word won't do you any good while it's on the pages of the Bible. God's Word must rise off the pages of the Bible and enter into your spirit (into your heart) before it will do you any good. It's not enough to have God's Word on paper. That won't do you any good in the everyday, hum-drum, rough and tumble, nitty-gritty world that we live in. You have to get God's Word off that page and into your spirit. YOU MUST KNOW, not think about it, you must know the reality of the Word of God.

I can analyze many Christians that I minister to day by day and week by week when they begin to talk to me. Right away they locate themselves by their words. They begin to talk and immediately my **computer** begins to analyze them, my **spectrograph** begins to check them out and I can tell what their problem is. **They don't know the reality of God's Word.** Oh, they believe God's Word; don't misunderstand me, they believe it. They believe in the Bible: they believe the Bible is God's Word, but **they don't know the reality of that Word in their own lives,** because they've never *acted* upon God's Word. They have never lived in God's Word. They just know it as something that sits on the mantelpiece or on the coffee table or on the night stand beside the bed, but the Word stays inside the Book, enclosed within those two covers.

You have to get that Word out of the Bible into you. In the natural, milk won't do you any good in the bottle. It has to get in you before it's going to nourish you. You can have a whole refrigerator full of milk and it will do you absolutely no good if you don't drink it. Perhaps you have a little baby. That baby feeds on milk. It wouldn't do any good to leave the refrigerator full of milk if none of it ever got into the baby. God's Word in the Book between the two leather covers won't do you any good, although it is true. Sure, there's milk in the refrigerator, all you have to do is open the door and you can see the bottles sitting there. The formula is made, the bottles are sitting in there cooling, ready to be used, but that by itself won't do the baby any good. It has to get out of the bottle and into the baby.

God's Word has to get out from between those two leather covers and *into your spirit*. You have to come to know God's Word as a living reality.

Too many Christians are trying to educate their minds first, and then let their minds educate their spirits. That is not the way God works. God works through the spirit of man. When man's spirit is brought into right relationship with God, and when man's spirit is fed properly on the Word of God, then man's spirit will educate man's mind and man's mind will bring man's body into subjection to the will of God.

The Word Of God Is A Living Thing—

In the book of Hebrews we find a very illuminating statement. We find a divine revelation about a truth that cannot be understood with the human intellect. It is a truth that must be received by your heart (spirit). It must be believed IN YOUR SPIRIT, then when it gets in your spirit it will educate your mind.

"For the word of God is quick, and powerful, and sharper than any twoedged sword, piercing even to the dividing asunder of soul and spirit, and of the joints and marrow, and is a discerner of the thoughts and intents of the heart" (Hebrews 4:12).

In the King James Version of the Bible the word *quick* is a very illusive word to us. We don't quite comprehend what it means; but in the Greek language, in which the New Testament was originally written, the word *quick* means *to make alive*. It means to make alive; it doesn't mean fast. Moffat's translation of the New Testament of this particular verse is translated like this: "For the Word of God is a living thing."

God's Word is ALIVE! Now it may be dead to you, but that's your problem. God's Word is alive and it will do exactly what God sent it to do. BUT, until it becomes a living reality in you, it won't do *you* any good. It may be true, but it won't do you any personal good until it gets in you.

Now he says the **Word of God is a living thing.** Well, if it is alive, then it can impart life. Living things perpetuate life. Living things have within them the ability and the potentiality to reproduce life. When something is dead, it doesn't give birth to life per se; but when something is alive, it has a capability to impart life.

God's Word can impart to us spiritual life, because the Word is alive. Too many Christians have very little regard for the reality of the living Word of God. If they really did, every time the doors of the church were opened it would be packed and jammed, for you know that God's Word says, "Not forsaking the assembling of ourselves together, as the manner of some is . . ." (Hebrews 10:25).

Now the question is: **Is it alive in you?** Until it does become alive in you, you will never have strong faith. You will not be able to exercise strong faith. Your faith will be weak. Your faith, strength-wise, will be like the little baby, weak and helpless, and totally dependent upon someone else.

I see this all the time. Christians come to me wanting to pray. They think that I have some super-duper spiritual magic, that God's not going to answer anybody else's prayer, only Fred's. "If I can just get Fred to pray, it'll work."

No, He's *your* Father too. Jesus is *your* Savior. He is not Fred's Savior alone, He's yours too. This is what I am striving to do, through this book. I want you to get to a point where you'll begin to believe in the reality of God's Word and then act upon it. I don't have any inside track to God. I don't have any corner on the market, spiritually. The Bible says that God is no respecter of persons. That means that He will hear you just as well as He will hear me.

I don't want to be a baby; I don't want to be dependent upon anybody in this world. I'm not going to be dependent upon anybody. I don't depend on anybody but God.

Now, don't misunderstand me, certainly people do things for me, and certainly I have to look to people to do things, but my faith and my final satisfaction is not in those people. I look beyond them and I see God. I trust God. I don't trust people to pay my wages. Sure, the money has to come through human hands. The Bible tells us that. "Give, and it shall be given unto you; good measure, pressed down and shaken together, and running over, shall men give into your bosom . . ." (Luke 6:38). Certainly the money comes through the hands of men, but I don't look to people as the source. I don't depend, as a pastor, upon whether or not we have a big crowd as to whether or not I'll get a paycheck. I'll get my money because the bank of heaven is solvent, glory to God! I'll get it because God will see to it. If only five people come to church on Sunday morning, I'll still get my money, because I am looking to God.

God's Word is alive, but is it alive in you?

Many times, we really don't have the appreciation for the Word of God that we ought to. Many people try to cop out by saying, "Well, you know the Bible was written by man!"

Who told you that? I mean, unless you were there when it was written, you're barking in the dark.

Listen to what God says about it. *"All scripture is given by inspiration of God, and is profitable for doctrine, for reproof, for correction, for instruction in righteousness: That the man of God may be perfect, throughly furnished unto all good works"* (II Timothy 3:16-17). The word *scripture* is another word for Bible or Holy Book, or Holy Writ, or Word of God. All of those terms are synonymous.

Look at verse 17 again. *"That the man of God,"* not the man of the world, but *"the man of God may be perfect,"* (fully spiritually mature). It doesn't mean flawlessness. The word *perfect* means spiritual maturity, full growth in spiritual matters. *"That the man of God may be perfect, throughly furnished unto all good works."*

All Scripture is given by inspiration of God. The Bible is God inspired. It is a living book. IT'S ALIVE!

Whether you believe it or not is irrelevant. It will live on. But, those who do believe the Bible and those who will get in step with it, will find out very quickly that God's Word is alive. When you realize that it is a living thing, and begin to act like it is true, you will break the shackles of weakness, doubt, and inability. You will begin to rise in the arms of strong faith and be able to move the hand of God.

You know you can never appreciate God, you can never fully love God, unless you love God's Word. You see, your love of God is based upon your love for His Word. If you don't love God's Word, you don't love God. I am going to prove that to you by His Word.

How To Love God—

For a long time it troubled me, how could I love God? I've never seen God. How could I work up feelings of love, feelings of affection for God when I had never seen Him? How could I work myself into a frame of mind where I could love God? Even after I had said the words, "God, I love You," it was just like talking to the ceiling because I couldn't see God. I couldn't touch God. I couldn't look into His eyes and see His expression when I told Him I loved Him. It was very difficult for me. I really went from here to yon, and back and forth, trying to figure out how I could work up a love for God.

Then one day I found in the Scriptures how I could love God. Ever since I discovered that, I've been the happiest person in the world. I don't have to work up any feelings. I don't have to get into some kind of a state of ecstasy, but I know I love Him. I know that my love for Him is accepted by Him because I found out HOW to do it, ON HIS TERMS. He gave me the answer! He gave me the secret, right here in His Word!

"He that hath my commandments, and keepeth them, he it is that loveth me: and he that loveth me shall be loved of my Father, and I will love him, and will manifest myself to him.

"Judas saith unto him, not Iscariot, Lord, how is it that thou wilt manifest thyself unto us, and not unto the world?

"Jesus answered and said unto him, If a man love me, he will keep my words: and my Father will love him, and we will come unto him, and make our abode with him.

"He that loveth me not keepeth not my sayings: and the word which ye hear is not mine, but the Father's which sent me" (John 14:21-24).

Love His Word—

Do you want to know how to love God?

Here is the secret. You have to **love His Word.** In the Greek the word *keep* doesn't mean what you think it means. You may think it means going and getting a lock of baby's hair and putting it with a picture of him inside your Bible, folding it between the pages to **save** it. Or maybe when Joe took you to the prom, or took you out on your anniversary and gave you a corsage, you put it in the Book and you pressed it down and every once in a while, you go back and look at it and it reminds you of twenty years ago.

See, that's what people usually think about the word *keep.* But that's not what it means in the Greek. The word *keep* is an action word that means **to do it.** It means to DO GOD'S WORD. When the Bible says "keep God's Word," it means to do God's Word. If you are not doing God's Word, Jesus says you don't love Him.

He said, "If you love me you will do my Words," not just on Sunday or Wednesday or Easter or Christmas or Thanksgiving, but seven days a week, three hundred and sixty-five and a quarter days a year.

Now, you say you love Him. What place does God's Word have in your life? If you don't **do** what this Word says, you are fooling yourself. Jesus said it! "If you love me, you'll keep my words." That means you'll do God's words, because you see, GOD'S WORD IS A LIVING THING.

In the following Scripture, Jesus is speaking and He makes this declaration: "It is the Spirit that quickeneth." There's that word *quicken* again. Remember that word means to make alive. He is saying, it is the Spirit that makes alive, that makes things living. He said, "It is the Spirit that quickeneth; the flesh profiteth nothing: the words that I speak unto you, they are spirit, and they are life" (John 6:63).

When Jesus said, "My words are spirit and they are life," what did He mean? What was He saying? He was saying, if we will accept His Word and believe His Word and digest His Word, it will cause or create spiritual life inside of us. And we will be able to live spiritually.

He didn't say, "My words are physical things." He didn't say, "My words are tangible things." He said, "MY WORDS ARE SPIRIT AND THEY ARE DIRECTED TO YOUR SPIRIT."

Most people try to receive God on an intellectual plane and they can't do that. There are many who are intellectually inclined, who have trained their minds very astutely. They have gone to the best universities and have sat at the feet of the best professors, and there is nothing wrong with that. I am not belittling that. But because of their intellectual training, when they come over into the realm of the things of the spirit, they are still trying to use the same paraphernalia to understand spiritual things. Jesus said, "My words are spirit and they are life. MY WORDS ARE SPIRIT AND THEY ARE LIVE."

Jesus' words are not intellectualisms, they're not philosophical ramblings; but His words are Spirit, and they are addressed to the spirit of man, to your inner man — not to your head, but to your heart.

Reader, you may be missing God because you are trying to figure God out with your intellect. You can't do it, because you're too limited. The human mind cannot contain God. God is too big for the human mind. God is so big that it says the heaven of heavens cannot even contain Him. God is so big that it says that you can't go under Him. He's so tall that you can't go over Him, and He's so wide that you can't go around Him. In other words, God is too big for the human mind. The Spirit is infinite.

God has created you a spirit being and it is only in the spirit that you can understand God. It is as your spirit is educated that your spirit can begin to educate your mind and your mind can learn how to act on God's Word instead of acting on logic or human reasoning.

Jesus said, "My words are spirit and they are life." When you feed upon the Word, when you know the reality of the fact that God's words are spirit and they are life, then they make you alive on the inside. They give you life on the inside. It's more than just a transcendent dream; it's more than something that comes for a moment of time. It is something that is lasting and vibrant. It's something that's scintillating, it's something that's palpitating, it's something that makes you warm on the inside. It is not an emotion, but a sense of the reality and the presence of God in your own spirit. The words that Jesus spoke when He said, "My words are spirit and my words are life," minister to your spirit.

Rise Up On The Eagle Wings Of Strong Faith—

Until you know the reality of the presence of God in your own spirit you'll never be able to exercise strong faith. You will never arrive at strong faith. You will be a weakling all of your spiritual life. You will be a victim of circumstances.

Far too many Christians are just that — victims of circumstances. They are beaten down by the waves of tribulation. They're beaten down by the winds of adversity. They're laid low by Satan and his demon host because they don't know how to rise up on the eagle wings of strong faith. They are down in the valley under the bushes, with weak faith, because they don't know the reality of God's Word. They haven't discovered that the words of God are spirit and they are life. They don't know that they can feed upon them and they will make them strong. When the forces of darkness come against them they can stand boldly and say, "I resist you in the Word, and in the name of Jesus," and those forces will have to come to an abrupt halt.

God's Word Will Set You Free—

There are so many Christians who dabble with the Word. There are many Christians who play with the Word as a little child plays with his vegetables; and most of the time he ends up throwing them on the floor. There are some who come to the Word and peck around like a little bird. Then, there are some who come like vultures and gorge themselves on the Word. They get fat and full. Some of them get so fat that they can't even get off the ground and fly! I know that that may sound like a negative analogy, but I think it illustrates a truth that we can see. You ought to gorge yourself on God's Word. You know that's the only thing that I see in the Bible that doesn't say that it's wrong to be a glutton about. It tells you about being a glutton about physical food, but nowhere does it even say to limit yourself on the Word of God. No! Just feed to your heart's content; it's good!

Have you tasted to see that the Word of God is good?

It's a living thing. IT'S ALIVE! God's Word imparts life to your spirit!

Not only is the Word of God alive, not only is it a living thing, but God's Word will set you FREE! Free from fears, hang-ups, inabilities, weaknesses, free from anything that holds you in bondage.

Some of you who read this book are in slavery to certain things. Perhaps you're in slavery to sex, or nicotine, drugs, or alcohol, whatever. You may **con** yourself and say, "Oh, I can quit any time I want to." If strong drink masters you, it's your ruler, and you are in bondage. You are just as addicted to that as a heroin addict is addicted to heroin. Some of you are in bondage to fear: You are afraid of height. You're afraid of the dark streets. You're afraid of a dark

house. You're afraid of this; you're afraid of that —
you are in bondage. Some of you are afraid of dying.
Right now, as you sit reading this book, you are
fearful of dying. It isn't just the old people either;
some young people are afraid of death.

I used to be afraid of death. Even after I became a
Christian I was afraid of death, because I didn't
understand it. I didn't know what the Living Word
said about it, and I was fearful about death. I wouldn't
fly in airplanes because I was afraid that the airplane
might crash and I would die at a young age. I didn't
want to die, so I wouldn't fly. I thought if I could stay
on the ground I would be safe! I feared death, because
I didn't know the living reality of the Word. Yes, I
believed in Jesus. Yes, I was saved. Yes, I was going
to heaven when I died, but I didn't have victory in this
life. You couldn't drag me on board an airplane — not
even at gunpoint!

Now, I can't wait until the next time to get on a
plane, because I know what to do. I know how to keep
it up in the sky. I don't rely upon the pilot; I don't rely
on the mechanics. If all the engines fall off, it will still
fly! I believe that. I am not just saying it. You see, I
know what the Word says. I've been freed from that
spirit of fear. I have been set free, because I know the
LIVING REALITY OF GOD'S WORD. I know that
His Word is spirit and it's life. I know that His Word
will sustain me, and I know that His Word will hold
me. I know that His Word will undergird me. I know
that I can stand on His Word and it's like standing on
a solid rock foundation. Though the winds may blow

around me and the winds may howl and scream, I can stand there and look them in the face and laugh at them, because HIS WORD IS ALIVE!

Jesus said in the 8th chapter of John, verses 31 and 32, *"Then said Jesus to those Jews which believed on him. IF* (underline the word if) *ye continue in my word* (not if you start in my Word, not if you dabble in it now and then) *then are ye my disciples indeed; And ye shall know the truth, and the truth shall make you free."*

Are you free?

When Jesus said, "If ye continue in my word," He meant an ongoing, constant, continuing in His Word. "If ye continue in my Word, then are ye my disciples indeed. And you (if you continue in my Word) will know the truth, and when you know the truth, you'll be made free."

You Don't Have To Be Sick—

When you know God's Word, when you have that literal Word down on the inside of you, you will find that you don't have to be sick. You'll find out that it's not God's will that you be sick. It is not God's will that you go through one day of your life being sick. The Bible says that one of God's seven redemptive names is **Jehovah Rapha, the Lord that healeth thee.** He didn't say, "I **was** the Lord that healeth thee." He didn't say, "I will be the Lord tomorrow, that healeth thee." He said "I AM THE LORD THAT HEALETH THEE" (Exodus 15:26).

When God told Moses at the burning bush to go down and tell Pharoah to let His people go, Moses said, "How can I go down there and talk to Pharoah? He's a great king of Egypt. I can't talk to him, I'm just a lowly sheepherder out here on the backside of a mountain. They don't know my name. They don't know who I am. When I go in there and tell them, what shall I say to them? Who shall I say sent me?"

God told Moses, "You tell them that I AM THAT I AM. (Exodus 3:14.) When I get through demonstrating my power, he'll let them go." God has never been, "I was." God is always, "I AM" — present tense. He is, whatever He is, right now. He is the Lord that healeth thee.

You don't have to be sick, but you see you won't know that truth until you know His Word. You must understand the reality of the Living Word of God.

In the Old Testament, when Israel became disobedient and backslid, when they were walking in sin and not following the commandments of God, Satan oppressed them and brought sickness and disease into the camp. God said, "If you'll turn to me, if you'll just look to me I'll send my Word and I'll heal you." When they turned to Him in repentance, the Bible says, *"He sent his word, and healed them . . ."* (Psalms 107:20). He didn't send healing, **He sent His WORD, and His Word healed them.**

Now, let's go over to the New Testament and look in the Gospel of John. We read in chapter 1, verse 1, *"In the beginning was the Word, and the Word was with God, and the Word was God."* Then, in the 14th verse it says, *"And the Word was made flesh, and dwelt among us . . . ."* God sent His Word again. He sent His Word to heal. When Jesus went out, the Bible says everybody who came near Him got healed. Even those who touched His garments were healed. His healing power flowed out of Him and healed them, because Jesus was God's Word sent to man to heal man. God is no less desirous that His children walk in perfect health now than He was then.

Under the Old Covenant He said, *"I'll take sickness out of the midst of thee, the number of thy days I will fulfill."* (Exodus 23:25-26.) He said all of that under the Old Covenant.

Under the Old Covenant they could have miracles, they could have good health, they could walk in strength and in power, and the Bible says that we have a better Covenant established upon better promises, and you mean to tell me that we have *less* under the New Covenant? If we do, then it's not as good as the Old.

No! Praise God. We have it now. God is still "I AM the Lord that healeth thee."

God Desires You To Be Rich—

If you continue in His Word, you'll know that He doesn't want you poverty stricken.

If you thought that man had you down, if you thought that man was trying to make you poor, you need to know it's been Satan, all along, camouflaging his actions and making you think it's the man across the street wanting to keep you down. You have to stay down yourself, in order to keep the other man down. That's ridiculous; it just looks like the man is keeping you down because the devil wants you to think that your enemy is the other man, instead of him. He cloaks his work in darkness and he hides behind that false appearance and tries to deceive you with it.

The devil is the one who desires you to be poor, but God desires you to be rich. To be rich means to be abundantly supplied.

Some of you readers can't even pay your rent. You are walking around crying. In fact some of you are living off the County. The King's children should not be dependent upon the County. You should thank the Lord for the County if you can't do any better. Thank God you don't have to starve to death. I'm not knocking that, but it's a shame that the King's children are dependent upon the County. If you are dependent upon someone else, it is because you don't know His Word. God's Word is not real and alive to you, and you think you have to make it on hand-outs. You need to know that the cattle on a thousand hills belong to your heavenly Father. (Psalm 50:10.) You need to realize that whatever belongs to the Father belongs to the child. The children eat out of the same refrigerator that the parents eat from. They sleep in the same house that the mother and father sleep in, don't they? They bathe in the same water that comes out of the same water heater that the mother and father bathe in, don't they?

Well, praise God! If my Father is rich then I ought to be rich! It isn't God who wants you poverty stricken. But, you see, if you don't know the Word, if you don't know the living reality of God's Word, then you will go through life in bondage to poverty.

Many Christians have this poverty syndrome. They think it's a mark of excellence to be poor. That's why many young people don't want to be bothered with Christianity, and I don't blame them. I will never forget an old man I knew once. I believe that old man was in his seventies or eighties. He was a spry old man; he was unusually spry to be so old. He could get around and did his work in the plant where he was employed better than many of the young guys in the plant, in terms of his ability and agility.

I tried to find a way that I could get to him and talk about the Word. I was looking for an opportunity to witness to the old man about Christ. One day, by virtue of the way the job was going, we were thrown together. I said, "Well, now I am going to talk to this old man about Christ and about his salvation."

As I began to talk to him, he turned to me and said, "Don't tell me anything about Christianity. I don't want to hear it. My father was a preacher, and we were so poor we didn't have food to eat. We didn't have shoes and we lived in the worst house. No, I don't need that."

He was a man who had money in the bank. He had saved up and he had worked hard. He didn't want anything to do with this "poverty thing." I couldn't blame him, but I couldn't say anything to him. I had to hang my head and say, "What can I do, what can I say?"

Here was a father, a preacher, who thought that it was right, thought that it was godly to be poor, thought that it was spiritual to have nothing, and because of this I couldn't reach his son.

Many young people think, *If I become a Christian, I can't do this, and I can't do that.*

Listen, if you are a Christian, you can have five Cadillacs if you can afford them. God doesn't care how many Cadillacs you have. You can have a Cadillac, a Mercedes, and a Rolls Royce all thrown in the same bag if you want. God is not opposed to that; He never has been.

Read your Old Testament. You will find that all of God's men were the richest men in the country. The Bible says that whatever He was, HE IS, and whatever HE IS, HE WILL BE. So, if He was God and He shined upon His children and they were rich *then* why should He want you poor *now?*

Abraham and his nephew Lot had so many cattle and so many flocks they couldn't even graze on the same countryside. Read your Bible! They had to split up and go in different directions, because the land wouldn't bear the cattle that they had. The cattle would have stripped the land naked, there were so many. They were rich, and they were God's men.

Solomon was so rich that it was unbelievable. God made Solomon rich, didn't He?

God Isn't Opposed To Us Having Things—

God is not opposed to us having things, HE IS OPPOSED TO THINGS HAVING US. There is a vast difference, friends. He doesn't want you seeking those things first. He wants you to seek Him first, and He will give you those things. The Bible says, "But seek ye first the kingdom of God, and his righteousness; and all these things shall be added unto you" (Matthew 6:33).

Notice **the Scripture does not say subtracted from you, but added unto you.** Get the rule: **seek first the kingdom of God.** That is where many make the mistake. They want to get the things first, and when they are secure in the things, then they say, "Now I can go to church. We have the children all off to college, and we have stocks and bonds. The dividends are flowing in. We have the house paid for (you're old and decrepit now), we can go to church now." You get there and you can't even hear the sermon, now your ears are going bad. "Ah, ah, what did he say, Momma? What did he say, huh?"

I'm not trying to be funny. I am trying to illustrate a point. Many Christians are like that. But you see, if you do what Jesus said, "If ye continue in my word, you'll know the truth," and you will find that you don't have to be poor. Praise God!

You have the riches of heaven behind you, because God is behind you. But you see, you can't know this unless you know the living reality of His Word.

You Continue In The Word—

Many Christians have never read the Bible. If someone asked you right now to find certain things in your Bible, would you know which direction to go to find the answer? Many people who have gone to church for years really don't know what the Word of God says about certain things. They are going on that emotion that they get every week. They are going on that sweet pill of emotion. When they get that pill, they figure they have been to church.

"Oh honey, we had a service today! Reverend really preached! Yes, we had a service today!"

"What did he preach about?"

"I don't know, but he sure did preach. Yes, he really preached!"

They have never opened their Bibles. They don't know the living reality of the Word of God. That's why they are living in the poverty syndrome. That's why they are sick and downtrodden. Then, the devil brings them that other lie and they accept it. "Well, now, you are sick to glorify God." They just go along and accept sickness because, "I'm glorifying God now."

Nowhere in the Bible can you find that God got any glory out of anybody being sick.

I'll tell you when He did get glory — when they got well. When they got healed, then the people glorified God!

When you continue in the Word, when you know the Bible, you will know that it says, "Himself took your infirmities and bore your sicknesses, and with His stripes you were healed." So, if you were healed, you are healed, and if you are, **you is.**

When you understand that and find it is a living reality, and you start to live like it's so, you will walk in perfect health! Praise God forevermore. You will walk in perfect health, because you see, the Word of God tells us, "Jesus Christ the same yesterday, and to day, and for ever" (Hebrews 13:8). And we have already read, "In the beginning was the Word, and the Word was with God, and the Word was God" (John 1:1). If the Word was God, then God was the Word. If Jesus was the Word, then Jesus is God and God is Jesus. Don't ask me how, because I don't know, but that's what the Bible says.

If Jesus is the same yesterday, today, and forever, then God must be the same yesterday, today, and forever. Everything He was yesterday, He is today; everything He was yesterday, He will be tomorrow; and everything He will be tomorrow, He will be forever, because the Scripture says, "He is the same yesterday, today, and forever." So, thank God, if He was Jehovah Rapha, the Lord that healeth thee, that means He wants you to be healed.

Use Your Free Will—

If you are sick, you can be well; but you will never be well unless you find it in the Word, believe it, and act on it. You have to get that Word built into your spirit so that you're operating on STRONG FAITH. Then you can receive healing for your body from the hand of God.

You don't have to go through life in pain and misery with arthritis, or all that. All of that is of Satan. It is not of God.

You say, "Yes, but I don't understand why God *allows* folks to be sick?"

Because you have a free will. USE it! You use it and go down and buy that six-pack when you want it, and you don't have to have any interpretation for it either. You just go down to the store and get it, isn't that right?

When you get that taste in your mouth, you go down there and say, "Give me a pack of cigarettes." It doesn't take you two minutes to do that, and you don't have to go to the preacher. "Well, what does this mean, pastor?" No, you just run down there and get it because you have a will. You do it because you **will** to do it. When you start **willing** to do God's will, you'll enter into that area where you will walk in the fullness of God's Word.

In **How To Obtain Strong Faith — Six Principles,** the first principle is: **You must Know the Reality of God's Word.**

Is God's Word real to you? Do you really know the living reality of the Word?

I thank God that His Word is so. You know for a long time I just *hoped* that the Bible was true. I wanted to believe it, but it was hard for me to do. I didn't know *how* to believe it.

People told me, "Oh, you have to pray harder."

I prayed harder but nothing happened. Then I read somebody's book that said, "Oh, you have to fast. If you go on a fast, you'll get it." I tried to fast and I got sick in the stomach. I went a day and I thought that I was going to die. Nothing happened.

Then somebody said, "Well, you know you have to go to church more." I went to church more, prayer meetings and everything. Nothing happened.

Then one day it dawned on me! One day the Spirit of God showed me! One day He said, "Just do what I say."

You can do it. Just act like God is talking to you and saying to you, "Hey, (*your name*), go do thus and so."

If God walked through your church door, clothed Himself in flesh, walked up to the pulpit, took His place behind the pulpit and said, "(*Your name*), go and do thus and so," my friend, would you wait for an interpretation? Would you wait to find out if this is according to your denomination? Or would you obey God?

Don't you know that the Bible is God's Word? It is as if God were standing there talking to you. It is just as valid, just as real as though God stood there and said, "Do it."

If you want to enter into strong faith, begin to get into the Word and devour it. Eat it and digest it everyday, just like you eat your regular food, and pretty soon that Living Word on the inside of you will come alive! You will begin to see that to do God's Word is to love God, to do God's Word is to please God, and to do God's Word is to have STRONG FAITH. Things will begin to pop for you! Things will begin to click for you and life will begin to take on that zest that God wanted it to have.

Yes, there'll be those who will call you a "fanatic!" There'll be those who will say, "Now, you're getting a little out of hand. You went to church three times last week!" There'll be those who will say, "You are praying too much, it's not good for the mind you know."

That's all right, let them do their talking. Let them talk all that stuff if they want to, but you ride on those eagle wings of faith, and enjoy the fullness of God. Rise above the smog of criticism, rise above those that would call you **a nut**. What a way to be a nut! Glory to God!

You now have principle number one — **you must Know the Reality of God's Word.**

2

Know the Reality of Your Redemption in Christ

As we continue our study on **How to Obtain Strong Faith — Six Principles,** I would like for you to realize that the Bible talks about degrees of faith.

There Are Degrees Of Faith—

The Bible talks about **weak faith;** the Bible talks about **strong faith;** the Bible talks about **great faith;** the Bible talks about **oh ye of little faith;** the Bible talks about **growing faith;** the Bible talks about **unfeigned faith;** and the Bible talks about **shipwrecked faith.**

You can see from these particular descriptive words that I have brought to your attention that there are degrees of faith. It is not just a matter of either having faith, or not having faith. It is a matter of you being at any one given time at one level or the other. You could be possessed of weak faith, or you could be possessed of strong faith.

The Bible tells us that it is those who have STRONG FAITH who obtain the promises of God. They are the ones who walk in the fullness of God's blessings. It is very important to you that you learn the principles of strong faith.

I am interested in the BIGGEST, the BEST, and the MOSTEST myself, in all things. I never shoot for the little things. I am always shooting for the big things because that is what my Father has taught me to do. My Father is BIG. I don't have a little Father. I don't have a weak Father. You see, I have a BIG FATHER. I have a great big wonderful God. Therefore everything about my Father is BIG!

I find in the Scriptures that it is those who have big or strong faith who obtain the promises of God.

Weak faith won't get much done, just as in the natural, weak things, little things won't get too much done. It is when faith is strong that you can obtain the promises of God.

God is a faith God; we must always keep that in mind.

We, as Christians, are children of God. We are faith children of a faith God. We are not emotional children of an emotional God.

You can be sure that if you want to please God, and if you are to obtain the promises of God, then you must do it through the avenue or through the channel of faith.

"But without faith it is impossible to please him; for he that cometh to God must believe that he is, and that he is a rewarder of them that diligently seek him" (Hebrews 11:6).

Too many times I have read in books (my library shelves are full of them, almost 700 volumes), that I need more faith. They told me that I need to pray more. They told me all of these things, but nobody told me HOW TO DO IT.

When you look in the mirror, you (pretty well) know what is wrong. It's not that you have the problem of knowing what's wrong with you; the problem is knowing how you can change what's wrong; how you can help get rid of what's wrong; or how you can fix what's wrong with you.

It's easy to throw a rock. Anybody can throw a rock through a plate glass window, but how do you establish that window? How are you going to get that big piece of glass in that window? That's the problem. Breaking it is no problem, just take a rock and throw it. What I am saying is, "It is easy to look and find fault, but do you know how to correct those faults?"

I believe that it is very important for you to understand how the principles work, and how you can apply them to your own life.

In this second chapter, we will discuss the second principle: You must **Know the Reality of your Redemption in Christ**, not as a creed, not as a denominational tenet, not as a traditional idea, not as some philosophical dissertation, but rather as a living reality.

You Must Know That You've Been Redeemed—

You are not in the process of being redeemed. You are not going to be redeemed off in the distant future, in the sweet by-and-by, pie in the sky. If you have been born again, you are redeemed NOW. You are redeemed.

Until you know that as a fact, as a reality, deep down in your own heart, you will never be possessed of strong faith. You will never be able to rise on the wings of strong faith and fly above the difficulties and the problems that surround you day by day. If you can learn to understand that Christ HAS MADE YOU FREE, you don't have to GET free; you don't have to ask anybody to SET you free: YOU ARE FREE IN CHRIST, then you are on your way to strong faith. When you are free in Christ, that freedom will flow over into every aspect or area of your life. You will find that once you realize that, not as a philosophy but as a fact, then nobody — but nobody — can keep you in bondage. Nobody can deny you the things that belong to you in this world or in the world to come, praise God!

In the book of Colossians there is a very important statement that bears heavy upon what we are talking about. It says this: "Giving thanks unto the Father, which hath made us meet to be partakers of the inheritance of the saints in light: Who hath delivered us from the power of darkness, and hath translated us into the kingdom of his dear Son: In whom we have redemption through his blood, even the forgiveness of sins" (Colossians 1:12-14). That word *meet* in the King

James Version of the Bible is somewhat misleading. The word simply means able. "Giving thanks unto the Father, which hath made us able to be partakers of the inheritance of the saints in light." Notice, He has made us ABLE to be partakers of the inheritance.

Be A Partaker—

The question is: Are you a partaker?

If you are not a partaker of the inheritance of the saints in light, then you are missing the blessing, and you are living below your privileges. You are living downstairs when you should be living in the penthouse!

Too many Christians are living downstairs in the cellar, when you ought to be living in the penthouse! Praise God, He wants you in the penthouse, and if you don't live there, that's on you. It's not on God because we just read, "Giving thanks unto the Father, which hath made us able to be partakers of the inheritance of the saints in light."

We also read in verses 13 and 14, "Who hath (has) delivered us from the power (that word *power* in the Greek means authority) of darkness, and hath translated us into the kingdom of his dear Son: In whom we have redemption through his blood, even the forgiveness of sins." God is not in the process of delivering us; He's not going to deliver us off in the future. The above scripture told us, "Who HATH delivered us." That word *hath* is past tense. That indicates that it is already done. God has already done it.

You say, "Yes, but I don't have the benefits of it. I don't feel like I'm very delivered." Well, that's your problem, friend. You need to find out what His Word says. If you will come to KNOW and understand what He has done for you, and then act like that's who you are, then you will begin to enjoy the benefits of your inheritance.

I praise the Lord, I am a recipient of it NOW. I'm enjoying it now and even the best is yet to come. I mean in this life, friend. I'm not talking about pie-in-the-sky, although I am going to have pie-in-the-sky, that's already a foregone conclusion. I have that in the bag. I am talking about right now — yes, right now.

Let's look at that scripture again. Notice he says, "Who hath delivered us from the authority of darkness." Now, the Bible says that God is light. Well, if God is light, then the opposite of God would be darkness, is that right? Therefore, if it says we have been delivered from the power (authority) of darkness, then that means we have been delivered from that which is opposed or opposite to God.

When we look into the Scriptures, we find that we do have an adversary. He would like for us to believe that he doesn't exist, but he is real. Satan is real. But, the Bible says that we have been delivered out of the authority of darkness.

Darkness Has No Legal Authority To Hold Us In Bondage—

Many things exist in life because we permit them to exist, not only in the spirit realm but also in the natural realm. For example, ecology. Everybody is all upset and uptight about the fact that the birds are becoming extinct. Many varieties of plants are being exterminated by smog and other things. Everybody is talking about ecology, but it's a simple thing to get rid of smog. We could clear up air pollution in the next six months if we really wanted to. We have the technology to clear it up. We just don't have the will to do it.

The whole problem is that it's a matter of the **will.** It isn't a matter of not knowing how to do it, but you see the greed for money keeps us in bondage. We would rather kill ourselves and cut our lives short by fifteen years or so, because we want a little more money in the bank.

When I say "we," I mean our society as a whole. We can get rid of the pollution if we want to. We know how to get rid of the slums. We could clear them out and there would be no more slums in America if we really wanted to do it. We don't want to do it!

We talk about how bad the situation is and yet these things exist because we *permit* them to exist. We could get rid of the smog; we could get rid of all the degradation that is going on in our country; and we could get rid of the slums if we *chose* to do it.

We can do anything we want to do. One day the President of the United States declared, "By such and such a date we will put a man on the moon," and we did it. Do you know why? We did it because we **willed** to do it. Our government put every facility that was available behind that project and they shot a man up there, 250,000 miles away, so he could collect a bag full of dust and rocks. They did that just because they wanted to do it. They determined that they would do it, and they had to make up new machinery. They had to create and invent new mechanisms to do it — but they did it because they WILLED TO DO IT.

Many things exist in our lives as Christians, just because we permit them to exist. Satan has his foot on the neck of so many Christians that it is pathetic. The reason that he does it is because they *permit* it, because we read in Colossians 1:13, "Who hath delivered us from the power (authority) of darkness . . . ." Satan is the power of darkness. He doesn't have any legal authority to hold us in bondage.

Darkness is Satan's kingdom. *"For we wrestle not against flesh and blood, but against principalities, against powers, against the rulers of the darkness of this world, against spiritual wickedness in high places"* (Ephesians 6:12).

That verse tells us right there that the enemy is not flesh and blood. Wrestling denotes contention; it denotes an opponent of some kind, isn't that right? But, your enemy is not the man who works at the bench next to you, or drives the truck in the same lot where you load your truck. It's not the man who sits in the same classroom with you. You think that man is the enemy, but that isn't true.

Look again at what Paul says, "For we wrestle not against flesh and blood, but against principalities, against powers, against the rulers of the darkness of this world, against spiritual wickedness in high places." It is more literally translated in the Greek, "wicked spirits in high or heavenly places."

The foe or the enemy that we have is a spiritual enemy, and he is characterized by darkness: ". . . *rulers of the darkness of this world.*"

If you didn't know it, I am telling you, this world is in darkness because of these wicked spirits, and they hold men in bondage. If you don't think that men are in bondage, just walk the streets of your city, go from one end of it to the other. Then multiply your city by thousands of other cities all over this country and all over the world. Men and women, boys and girls, in the bondage of starvation, in slavery to narcotic addiction, alcohol, nicotine, sex, fear and many other things.

Act On It—

The Bible tells us that Jesus Christ has redeemed us from this authority, that these things do not have any legal right to hold us in bondage. We have been redeemed. But until you know that as a living reality, until you begin to say it with your mouth, and believe it in your heart, and begin to ACT like it is so, these wicked spirits that are in the kingdom of darkness will enslave you. They will hold you in bondage, in the bondage of prejudice, hate, and malice.

The Word of God says we've been set free. WE ARE FREE! No man can hold you in bondage. No situation or circumstance or condition can hold you in bondage, for the Bible says that God's Word is forever settled in heaven, therefore it cannot fail.

It won't work for you until you *believe it, act on it,* and *confess it.* That's the difference. Many things are true but they won't help you unless you **act on those things.** You must do what is necessary to receive these things from God. Things are not just so because there is a pronouncement made about it. It may be legally true, but that doesn't make it true for you until you act on it, until you take advantage of it.

The Twofold Key—

"And there was war in heaven: Michael and his angels fought against the dragon; and the dragon fought and his angels.

"And prevailed not; neither was their place found any more in heaven.

"And the great dragon was cast out, that old serpent, called the Devil, and Satan, which deceiveth the whole world: he was cast out into the earth, and his angels were cast out with him.

"And I heard a loud voice saying in heaven, Now is come salvation, and strength, and the kingdom of our God, and the power of his Christ: for the accuser of our brethren is cast down, which accused them before our God day and night.

"AND THEY OVERCAME HIM BY THE BLOOD OF THE LAMB, AND BY THE WORD OF THEIR TESTIMONY" (Revelation 12:7-11).

This is the twofold key to operating and exercising and enjoying the fullness of this redemption that is in Christ, the fact that we have been redeemed from the powers and the kingdom of darkness.

But you see, **that as a stated fact** won't do you any good personally until **you add your testimony** to it. **You** have to **confess** that **it's true.** You have to say, **I have been redeemed.** You have to say, **I am not in bondage to the powers of darkness, to these wicked spirits. I have been made free by the blood of Christ. I have been redeemed from the curse of the law. I have been set free!**

It won't work for you until you confess it with your mouth, and then act like it's so in your life. It's not enough to have it on the pages of your Bible. It's not enough for you to read it on the pages of this book. You have to get it into your heart and you have to get it into your mouth. YOU HAVE TO BELIEVE IT WITH YOUR HEART, AND START SAYING IT WITH YOUR MOUTH. Then it begins to work on your behalf, and not until then. You have to realize that there is a reality here, that you have been redeemed and you are free.

You say, "Yes, but I don't feel free."

Do you know why?

Because you're not *acting* like you are free! ACTING on God's Word is faith. That's really all it is.

It's very simple. Faith is merely acting on what God says, just like you act on the word of a friend, just like you act on the word of your boss. You do all of that by faith.

Many of you readers are going to rise up early on Monday morning. Some of you will get up even before the sun comes up. You are going to get up out of that nice warm bed, get yourself all together, get into your car and drive down the streets to your job. You will put in eight long hours of your life, and Tuesday you'll put in eight more, and again Wednesday and so on. You do all of this on *the word of a man.*

He told you that if you put in forty hours he will pay you "X" number of dollars, and you trot right down there and do it. I ask you, when you hired in on the job that you work on, did you take with you a certified public accountant and have him check out the books of the company to see if they had enough money in the bank to pay you at the end of the week?

You never did that. You just believed what the man told you and you went to work. That's faith. That's what faith is — just acting on the word of someone, doing what his word said.

That is over in the natural realm, but the principle is identically the same in the realm of spiritual things.

It is just as simple as going to work. You believe that man and you act on his word. He tells you to come to work and you do it. You have no guarantee that you are going to get paid. Worse than that, we have some school teachers who work for a whole

month and don't get any money. They are doing it on
faith. That is the rule. They are acting on the word of
the one who is in authority.

In the spiritual realm, we act on what God says in
the Bible (His Word). If He tells you you are
redeemed, then you ought to act like you are
redeemed. If you have a job and you are going to that
job tomorrow, you don't go home and sit on the couch
and say, "Oh, I wonder where I am going to get the
money. I don't know what I am going to do about a
job. Oh, I wish I had a job. I have bills to pay and the
kids need clothes and food. What am I going to do?"

If you have a job, you don't do that. You have a
job and you ACT like it. You are confident. You just
assume that you are going to be paid; you act on the
man's words. You say, "Well, tomorrow morning I'll get
up and go to work." You don't make any great plans
about it. It's a fact and you just act like it's so.
You may go down to the furniture store and say to the
salesman, "I want a new television or a new couch, a
refrigerator and stove." You just walk in. You don't
even have any money in your pocket, but you say,
"That's the one I want right there. Make it green. I'll
take that washer and dryer, too."

The salesman is just writing it all down. "Sign
right here, please!" You may put a few dollars down,
maybe not. You know you will pay extended payments
on what you have chosen, and you don't even have the
money yet.

When you do this, you are acting on the fact that you have a job. That's faith in the natural world.

Faith in the spiritual world works the same way. God tells you that if you are saved you're redeemed from the powers of darkness, that He has set you free. Then YOU JUST ACT LIKE YOU ARE FREE! Because you are free indeed!

When something comes that would put you in bondage, simply say, "No, I can't do that, I am free. You can't put that on me." It is the same principle: you believe God's Word just as you believe your friends.

Many of us as Christians miss it because we're so conditioned to logic that we have to figure everything out. When we come to the things of the spirit, we just know that this must be even more technical than launching a missile. But it is so simple that people stumble over it. Thank God we've been redeemed!

Add Your Testimony—

These people overcame the enemy by the word of their testimony and by the blood of the Lamb. The blood of the Lamb has secured for us the redemption from the powers of darkness.

When you take in your mouth that WORD and begin to confess that that's who you are — one of the redeemed — you will break the shackles of the enemy. You say, "I'm free, you can't hold me in bondage. You can't stop one single dime from coming to me, not a dime; because I've been redeemed. I'M FREE!"

I may sound like a nut to some people, but I couldn't care less what they think. It never bothers me what they think. They can't stop the sun from coming up one day. No, what they think doesn't matter to me. I am only concerned about what my Father says.

I am doing what the Word says. The WORD tells me that I have been set free! I have been redeemed! Now it says that, "By the word of their testimony, and by the blood of the Lamb they overcame."

That is how you are going to have to overcome, by adding your testimony to what the Word says. The Word says He has redeemed you and has set you free from the authority of darkness.

When you start adding your testimony to that by confessing, "This is who I am; this is what I have," then it will start working on your behalf. Until you do that, you will be in bondage. I have to keep restating this because I find that it's difficult for people to comprehend it. They don't get it because they are trying to rationalize it out in their minds. It is not reasonable to your mind. It's not addressed to your mind. It's addressed to your spirit or to your heart.

When you can pick it up in your heart (spirit), your spirit can then educate your mind. But we go at it in the reverse order. We try to get our minds educated on these things and then we think that we can make it work. It doesn't work that way.

"Wherefore I also, after I heard of your faith in the Lord Jesus, and love unto all the saints, Cease not to give thanks for you, making mention of you in my

prayers; That the God of our Lord Jesus Christ, the Father of glory, may give unto you the spirit of wisdom and revelation in the knowledge of him. The eyes of your understanding being enlightened; that ye may know what is the hope of his calling, and what the riches of the glory of his inheritance in the saints, And what is the exceeding greatness of his power to usward who believe, according to the working of his mighty power, Which he wrought in Christ, when he raised him from the dead, and set him at his own right hand in the heavenly places, Far above all principality, and power, and might, and dominion, and every name that is named, not only in this world, but also in that which is to come: And hath put all things under his feet, and gave him to be the head over all things to the church, Which is his body, the fulness of him that filleth all in all" (Ephesians 1:15-23).

Are you a believer?

If you are a believer, Paul is talking to you. Let's find out what he is talking about when he says, *"to usward who believe."* Let's read it again — "To usward who believe, according to the working of his mighty power, Which he wrought in Christ, when he raised him from the dead, and set him at his own right hand in the heavenly places," watch this now, "Far above all principality, and authority (That's what that word *power* means, *authority and might*), "and dominion, and every name that is named, not only in this world, but also in that which is to come: And hath put ALL THINGS under his feet, and gave him to be the head over all things to the church, Which is his body, the fulness of him that filleth all in all."

The Church is His body. If the Church is the body of Christ, and if God has raised Christ from the dead and placed Him at His own right hand, far above all principality, all authority, all might, all dominion, and every name that is named, and if He is the head of the Church and we are the body (we are His body), then let me ask you: Where are your feet located? In your head or in your body?

Where are your feet in the natural? Your feet are attached to your body. Now, let's look at verse 22 again, *"And hath put all things under his feet."* Now watch this: If we are the body, and He is the head, then that means that our feet are located in the body. If God has put all things under the feet of Christ, and we are the body of Christ, and the feet are located in the body, then that means that all things are under OUR FEET!

That is saying the very same thing that He said in Colossians when He said, "He has redeemed us from the authority of darkness." He has taken us out from under it and has placed us at the right hand of the majesty on high.

That means that everything and all things are under my feet. If that is true, that means I am on top and things are on the bottom. Isn't that right?

If I am on top, how can I be defeated?

If I am on top, all I have to do is act like I'm on top. I have to act like what I am saying, and what the

Word is saying, is true. Just like you do when you go to work tomorrow morning on the word of a man, and put in eight long hours on nothing else than the word of a man.

Can you believe God's Word? Then ACT ON THE WORD OF GOD!

God's Word Never Changes—

A man's word can change, but the Bible says that God doesn't change. He's the same yesterday, today and forever. Whatever He was yesterday, whatever He is today, whatever He is tomorrow, He will be forever. He never changes. (Hebrews 13:8; Malachi 3:6; Romans 3:4)

Praise God, HIS WORD DOES NOT CHANGE. He said, "Till heaven and earth pass, one jot or one tittle, shall in no wise pass from the law, till all be fulfilled" (Matthew 5:18).

"*. . . For ever, O Lord, thy word is settled in heaven*" (Psalm 119:89).

"*My word . . . shall not return unto me void, but it shall accomplish that which I please and it shall prosper in the thing whereto I sent it*" (Isaiah 55:11).

"*I will hasten* (or watch over) *my word to perform it*" (Jeremiah 1:12).

"*Thou hast magnified thy word above thy name*" (Psalm 138:2).

All the above scriptures are in God's Word, but you have to act on them. You will act on the word of a weak, faulty human; why won't you act on God's Word?

All you have to do is say, "All things are under my feet," and then start acting like all things are under your feet.

You say, "But you just don't understand how hard I am having it. You just don't know all the problems that I have at home."

Well, you just told me what is wrong. You just said it: "All MY problems." You said YOU HAD THEM, didn't you?

All you have to do is get rid of them, then you won't have them. Say, "I believe I am free of all problems."

People say, "Aw, he's just lying; he's got problems just like everybody else."

No, I don't have any problems because the Bible tells me that *all things* are under my feet. That means the problems too.

Perhaps the difference between you and me is that I am just acting like it.

You may say, "Yes, but you are just acting like a fool. That doesn't make sense."

Well, I would rather be a fool and be free, than be wise like you and in bondage.

He said, "ALL THINGS." The reason that all things are under our feet is because we have been redeemed from the authority of darkness. Those powers have no legal right to hold us in bondage.

They will hold you in bondage if you allow them to. Yes, they will hold you in dire bondage, if you let them. But if you, by the word of your testimony, take God's Word into your mouth and break the power of Satan over your life, you can be free!

Someone said, "Sometimes God puts these things on us, these burdens and problems, these crosses to make us humble."

Well, that is a bald-faced lie. That is not the Bible, but many Christians believe that. They think, "Well, I'm sick so God can get the glory. I'm going to struggle through it and after awhile, by and by, I'll put on my long white robe and walk the golden streets."

NO! The Word says all things are under my feet. That means all the crosses and everything else is under my feet.

He didn't say *some* things. He didn't say the big things or the little things. HE SAID ALL THINGS. You have been redeemed! Start acting like that's true.

Until you know that as a living reality in your life, you can never exercise strong faith, because you'll never be sure where you are. You will always be wondering, "Does God really love me? Is God going to bless me? Is He going to hear my prayer?"

Thank God, I know He hears every prayer I pray; not some of the time, but all of the time. The reason I know that is because He told me so! He told me, "And this is the confidence that we have in him, that, if we ask any thing according to his will, he heareth us" (I John 5:14). It's just that simple.

We Are The Sons Of God—

Now, we see that we've been redeemed. We know that all things are under our feet. We understand that we must add the testimony of our lips to that which God's Word declares. Let's find out how God sees us. "Behold, what manner of love the Father hath bestowed upon us, that we should be called the sons of God . . ." (I John 3:1).

We are the sons of God. We have been redeemed from the kingdom of darkness, and it has no legal right to hold us in bondage to anything.

I refuse to be under bondage to anything. I didn't say I was perfect, don't get that idea. If you are looking for a perfect preacher, you've missed it. I'll tell you that right now. Don't look too closely at me because you will find a lot of flaws. I don't claim to be perfect.

I'm just like the Apostle Paul. Paul said, *"Brethren, I count not myself to have apprehended (or am already perfect): but this one thing I do, forgetting those things which are behind, and reaching forth unto those things which are before, I press toward the mark for the prize of the high calling of God in Christ Jesus"* (Philippians 3:13-14).

If you are running around trying to find a perfect church, with perfect people, you aren't going to find it. Sure, things are going on that may not be just right, but I don't care what's going on. I'm not going to worry about it. If it comes out in the open and it is hindering the WORD, I'll pounce on it just like a lion on a lamb. But, if folks are not living right, that's their problem, not mine. I'm not God. If they want to come to church and be sanctimonious, and then go out and do all their devilment in the world, that's their problem not mine. They don't answer to me. They'll answer to the Man though. Don't you know what the Church is on earth? The Church is God's laundry on earth. Now, whoever heard of taking clean clothes to the laundry?

No, you take dirty clothes to the laundry to get them cleaned. Isn't that right? That's what the Church is for — to clean us up. We're getting cleaner day by day, week by week, and month by month! None of us have arrived yet. None of us are perfect yet. If you are holding back, and staying back on the fringes of the crowd, not wanting to get in too close for fear of finding out something about somebody, I'll tell you right now, we are all in the same bag together. None of us are perfect.

I'll tell you what you can do. I'll tell you just like Jesus told those rascals who stayed up all night, finding that poor woman committing adultery. The dirty dogs, they wouldn't even bring the man in; like a woman could commit adultery by her lonesome. They brought the woman in and said, "Now the law says she ought to be stoned. What do you say about it?"

Jesus stooped over and started writing on the ground, He straightened up and said, "Boy, you guys are right. Fellows, you're right. I tell you, you hit the nail right on the head. I'll tell you what we are going to do. We are going to stone her. You're right, she ought to be stoned. I'll tell you what, he that is without sin, you throw the first rock. You pick up the first stone and throw it."

And you know what the Bible says: "They started creeping out, one by one; one by one they began to step out." Jesus went back to writing on the ground. He stood up again, and said, "Woman, where are thine accusers, hath no man condemned thee?"

She said, "No Lord, no man."

He said, "Neither do I condemn thee, go in peace and sin no more."

No, we haven't arrived yet, but we are working on it. In I John 3:8 it says, *"He that committeth sin is of the devil; for the devil sinneth from the beginning. For this purpose the Son of God was manifested, that he might destroy the works of the devil."*

Hallelujah, we've been redeemed! The works of Satan have been destroyed. The word *destroy* in the Greek means "to loosen or to dissolve, to sever, to break or demolish." It means "to loosen, especially by way of deliverance." So what it litterally means is that Jesus has taken the authority of Satan and all of his demonic forces and all of those in the kingdom of darkness and broken their authority over the Church, His Body.

Satan does have dominion in the world. Satan is still ruling the world with an iron hand, but he doesn't rule in the lives of Christians, or I should say, **he doesn't have any legal right to rule in the lives of Christians.**

All you have to do to stop him, when he comes in with his lies and temptation, is merely hold up your hand in the name of Jesus, and say, "Satan, your power's been broken. Jesus has loosed your power. You have no authority over my life," and he'll pack his bags and leave.

Use Your Authority—

If you don't know that, and if you don't use the authority that Jesus has given you, if you don't say it with your mouth, he will hound you and bug you and make your life hell on earth.

When you find out the fact that God's Word says that we have been redeemed, and that all things are under our feet, and you ACT like it, then by adding your testimony to the Word of God, things will begin to happen on your behalf.

Sickness and disease will leave, praise God! Sickness is of Satan. Sickness is of the devil, to bind men and to keep them in bondage. I'm against sickness 115%! I'm against disease and sickness because it's not of God, it's of Satan, and anywhere and everywhere I find it, I challenge it, and go against it in the name of Jesus.

Remember, we are talking about **How To Obtain Strong Faith — Six Principles.**

Do you want strong faith?

Praise God! I don't want anything weak. I don't want weak faith. I want STRONG faith, because that's the kind of faith that moves the hand of God.

YOU are the temple of God. Your body is the temple of God.

"Know ye not that ye are the temple of God, and that the Spirit of God dwelleth in you? If any man defile the temple of God, him shall God destroy; for the temple of God is holy, which temple ye are" (I Corinthians 3:16-17).

"What? know ye not that your body is the temple of the Holy Ghost which is in you, which ye have of God, and ye are not your own? For ye are bought with a price: (that price was the redemptive blood of Christ) *therefore glorify God in your body, and in your spirit, which are God's"* (I Corinthians 6:19-20).

How can you glorify God in your body when your body is malfunctioning? How can you glorify God when your body is eaten up by cancer or by T.B. or by some other vile disease? How can you glorify God in your body when your eyes are not properly functioning, when your ears are not properly functioning. How can you glorify God?

Notice, it says that our bodies are the temple of God. God is not going to dwell in a broken-down, ramshackled, leaky-roofed temple. God is going to live in a beautiful temple.

That's one of the things I can say about pagan religions. If you ever go to their places of worship, you will see that they have the most beautiful temples. They may be in starvation but the temples for their god are beautiful things to behold. Nothing is too good for their god.

Well, God lives and dwells in the most intricate, the most beautiful, the most perfectly designed temple in the universe — the human body. There's no mechanism, no house, no building, no machine like the human body. And the reason that it is so complex and beautiful, in all its vast intricate functionings, is because it is the place that God made for himself to live.

The Bible says, *"Be ye not unequally yoked together with unbelievers: for what fellowship hath righteousness with unrighteousness? and what communion hath light with darkness? And what concord hath Christ with Belial? or what part hath he that believeth with an infidel? And what agreement hath the temple of God with idols? for ye are the temple of the living God, as God hath said, I will dwell in them, and walk in them; and I will be their God, and they shall be my people"* (II Corinthians 6:14-16).

We are righteousness. We are light. We are Christ. We are believers.

We **give** the enemy the victory when we allow him to lord it over our lives, not only in the spiritual realm, not only the soulish realm, but also in the physical realm.

We should be the masters of our circumstances. We should be the victors of our environment. We should be on top and all things should be under our feet, because the Bible says that's so.

Now, what you have to do is start adding your testimony to that; you have to start confessing it. You have to start saying that this is who you are, and this is what you have, because God has given it to you. When you start *acting* like that's who you are, I'll guarantee you things will start clicking for you. Things will start working for you. Things will begin to come to you and you will begin to rise above the clouds as it were and walk on the high places in STRONG FAITH.

3

Know the Reality of the New Creation

As we continue our study of **how to Obtain Strong Faith — Six Principles,** I trust that you understand the first two principles that we covered in chapters one and two of this book.

Principle number one: **You must Know the Reality of the Word of God.** God's Word is Spirit; God's Word is life. You must get into the Word; continue in the Word; devour it; get it down into your spirit, so that you may know the living reality of God's Word.

Principle number two: **You must Know the Reality of your Redemption in Christ.** You must **know** that **you have been redeemed.** You are **not going to be redeemed.** You are **not in the process of being redeemed,** but the Bible tells you that (if you have accepted Jesus as your Lord and Savior) **you have been redeemed.**

You need to know that as an actual, spiritual, Biblical fact. Until you know that as a fact, down on the inside of you, in your spirit, you will never be able to obtain STRONG faith, because you will always have a low estimate of yourself. Satan will feed that low estimate, and you'll never be able to rise to the level of strong faith.

The next principle that we want to talk about is: **You must Know the Reality of the New Creation.**

You must know this not as an idea, not as a philosophy, not as a creed, not as a figment of someone's imagination, not as a denominational pronouncement, but you must *KNOW the FACT that YOU have been made a new creature in Christ.* That knowledge will have a tremendous influence upon the way you live.

Many Christians live a life that is below standard. They live a life below their rightful privileges in Christ, because they do not understand or realize that they have been made new creatures. They think they are still the way they used to be. They have not understood that they are new creatures.

Learn To See Yourself As God Sees You—

You need to learn how to see yourself as God sees you. You should not see yourself as Satan sees you. You should not see yourself as other men see you, but you should see yourself as God sees you. Until you learn to see yourself as God sees you, you will never be able to obtain strong faith. You will always live a life that is defeated spiritually, and you will never rise to your rightful blood-bought privileges. You must **see yourself as God sees you—A NEW CREATURE IN CHRIST.**

Let's examine what the Word of God says about us. You must keep in mind that when we call your attention to these particular scriptures, we are showing you God's estimate of you, how God sees you.

"Therefore if any man be in Christ, he is a new creature: old things are passed away; behold, all things are become new" (II Corinthians 5:17). Are you in Christ? The scripture says that if you are in Christ you are a new creature. One translation says that you are a "new creation." Another translation says that you are a new "species," you've never existed before; you are a brand new species, if you are in Christ.

When it says, "old things are passed away; behold, all things are become new," you must understand, "all things" refers to all things in the spirit realm, not all things in the natural. In other words, not all things in the body are new. You are the same as you always were in the flesh. That is why you're still tempted. That's the reason you can still yield to temptation; your body is the same as it always has been. It has not been redeemed yet.

The Price Has Been Paid—

The Bible says that we are waiting for the redemption of our bodies. The price for the redemption of our bodies has been paid, but physically it hasn't happened yet. When Jesus comes back our bodies will be changed and made like unto His glorious body. If we are dead and our bodies are in the grave, our bodies will be resurrected and made like His glorious body.

Your Spirit Man Is The New Creature—

It's not your body that's new, it is your spirit man. You are a new creature in the spirit, the inner man. The spirit, the inner man, is the man that has to respond to God.

God is a Spirit. Man is a spirit. He has a soul, and he lives in a body. God deals with man through his spirit nature. The above scripture told us that we are new creatures in Christ Jesus. We have been made new in Christ, in the spirit man.

Please keep in mind that I want you to see yourself as God sees you. That's what is important. Even in the natural realm it is important. You may work on a job and you may think you're the world's greatest typist. You may think you're burning up the keyboard. You may think that you ought to be the chief typist in the typist pool, that you are the **top dog,** but do you know that your raises or promotions are not based so much upon how you see yourself, but on how your boss sees you? You may think you're the world's greatest, but that doesn't make too much difference. It is what the man who signs the payroll checks and puts in the promotions thinks about you that counts. You need to live in such a way, and do your work in such a way, that when that man sees you, he can evaluate you and give you the reward that you rightfully deserve.

It works the same way in things of the spirit. It isn't too important what you think about me. It isn't too important what I think about you. What really counts is what God thinks about us.

How does God see you?

Your works and all that you do should be done with a single eye toward pleasing God. He is the one who has the power to reward you. God is the one who has the power to promote you.

What Counts With God Is A New Creature—

Galatians 6:15 says, *"For in Christ Jesus neither circumcision availeth anything, nor uncircumcision, but a new creature."* In other words, it doesn't make any difference whether you are circumcised or not circumcised as far as God is concerned. What counts is a new creature. That's what counts with God, a new creature, a new creation. Not whether you're circumcised, not whether you're baptized in Jesus' name or baptized in the name of the Father, the Son, and the Holy Ghost, or whether you're baptized at all. It is the new creature that counts with God.

If a man is in Christ, the Word says that he is a new creature and that's what counts. Now, you ought to do the other things. You ought to be baptized in water, but that is not what saves you. If that's what saves people, all we would have to do is go out and baptize everybody and they would be saved.

That scripture said, *"For in Christ Jesus neither circumcision availeth anything, nor uncircumcision, but a NEW CREATURE."* In Christ what counts is that you are a new creature.

Now, you must begin to see yourself as a new creature on the inside and then govern yourself accordingly.

Remember, principle number three is this: **You must Know the Reality of the New Creation.** This is not an idea in the mind, this is an actual fact — it is a reality. When you realize that you are a new creature in Christ Jesus, it can make all the difference in your spiritual life. It can make the difference between whether you live victoriously or whether you just live on the common ground of tradition.

All some people are interested in is just to live life like it has always been, just to be the same as they were 20 years ago.

I am disturbed if I can't see growth in myself between last week and this week. I get very disturbed when I look at myself six months ago and then look at myself today, if I see no change. If I see myself on the same level, I get very disturbed. I have to see growth. I thank God that I know I am growing. My knowledge is growing, my understanding is growing, my sensitivity is growing to the things of God, and I can see that.

Some people I know are the same as they were seven years ago when I first met them, spiritually speaking. Some of them are just like they were three years ago. There is no change in them.

If you aren't growing spiritually, and you're happy with that, I guess if the Lord can stand it, I can!

You don't have to stay the same. You can grow and know that you are growing. You can become stronger in faith, you can become more knowledgeable in the things of God.

You can walk closer to God. In fact, if you keep walking just right, you may do just like Enoch. You may just walk right on into heaven! If it happened once, it could happen again, right? Enoch walked with God and he just took off and walked right on into glory. Praise God! No death, no funeral, he just walked right on into glory!

In the gospel of John we have the account of Jesus when He was talking to the man, Nicodemus. Nicodemus had come to Jesus and with flattering words had said to Him, *"We know that thou art a teacher come from God: for no man can do these miracles that thou doest, except God be with him"* (John 3:2).

Jesus cut right across all of that and went right to the heart of the matter, and He said in the 3rd verse, *". . . Verily, verily* (or truly, truly), *I say unto thee, Except a man be born again, he cannot see the kingdom of God."*

Those words "born again" literally mean "born anew" or "born from above." The word *see* means to come to know, or to come to understanding about the kingdom of God. It doesn't mean to visually see it with your natural eyes, like you see a person, but it means to come to *know* or *understand* the kingdom of God. You can't do it until you've been born again, or born anew.

You see, when man is first born, he is born in sin. He has to be born out of sin and he has to be born into the Body of Christ, or into the family of God. He has to be born again.

Adam was created and then he sinned. He died spiritually, and because we are his offspring, we inherit his spiritually dead nature. So, in order for us to relate to God, we have to be born out of that spiritually dead nature. We have to be born again so that we can be made alive spiritually.

Jesus is telling Nicodemus, "Except a man be born again," or unless he's born anew, "he cannot see the kingdom of God," he cannot come to know it.

Being born again is a spiritual transaction. It has nothing in the world to do with your flesh. It says in the 6th verse of that same chapter, *"That which is born of the flesh is flesh: and that which is born of the Spirit is spirit."*

Notice, He did not say, that which is born of the spirit is flesh; it did not say that which is born of the spirit is soul, but it said, "That which is born of the flesh is flesh." All that flesh can do is reproduce flesh, and He said, "That which is born of the Spirit is spirit."

What Jesus is saying is that the new birth is the rebirth of the human spirit. The flesh remains the same, but it is the spirit that is made new. The spirit is the one that's been created in Christ Jesus, a new creature, that man on the inside.

Now It's Up To You—

Now it's up to you to do something about the man on the outside, about the flesh or the body. It is necessary that you understand that you are sons of God if you have been born again. You are legally sons of God, and because you are legally sons of God, then you have a legal right to everything that God has. It belongs to you.

Everything that I have, my children have. They have a right to it. They don't have to pay for it. All they have to do is ask for it. God does that and that's why He tells us, "Ask, and it shall be given you: seek, and ye shall find; knock, and it shall be opened unto you" (Matthew 7:7). He didn't say it **might be opened.** He didn't say **there's a chance** you'd find. He said **seek** and **you will find.** He said **ask** and **you will receive.** Well, in reverse order, it says if you don't ask, you won't receive; and if you don't seek, you won't find; and if you don't knock, the door won't be opened.

You see, you are legally a son of God, and because you are legally a son of God, then you have a legal right to everything that heaven has to offer.

When Christians understand that, they will come out of the poverty syndrome; they'll come out of the sickness bag, and they will begin to walk on the high places of STRONG FAITH. They will begin to exercise their blood-bought rights — their legal rights — and they will begin to break the shackles of darkness and sin, sickness and poverty, and spiritual death, and

Satan and demons. They will begin to exert their sonship and live in this life as sons of God should live.

You're Legally God's Child If You're Born Again—

You need to understand that you are legally a son of God. It has nothing to do with how you *feel* about it. It is so because it's legally true. It doesn't matter how you feel.

Sometimes, my daughters can look so happy, they look like sunbeams — shining and glistening; and in 15 minutes they can look like a cloudy sky. But you know, whether they are sunshiny or cloudy they are still my children. Whether they feel good or bad, they still have a right to go into the refrigerator and eat whatever they want, because they are still my daughters, regardless of how they feel. All they have to do is come and get it, isn't that right?

Why?

Because legally they are my children and legally I have to take care of them.

You are God's legal child. He wants to take care of you. But don't you know that you can't take care of your children unless they let you. **God can't take care of you unless you let Him.**

Some of you won't let God take care of you. That's why He can't do anything even though He wants to. God cannot MAKE you accept anything. You have to receive it on your own, by faith.

Jesus told Nicodemus, "Except a man be born again, he cannot come to know the kingdom of God." The natural man and his natural mind with his natural logic cannot understand the things of the Spirit of God. Neither can he know them. They are foolishness to him because they are spiritually discerned. The natural mind cannot come to know the things of the Spirit of God. Only your reborn spirit can come to know the things of the Spirit of God, so understand — you are legally a son of God.

Let's look in the Bible and see something else that I believe is of infinite importance to us. Colossians 1:18 says, *"And he (Jesus) is the head of the body, the church: who is the beginning, the firstborn from the dead; that in all things he might have the preeminence."*

Please notice, Jesus Christ is the head of the body, the Church, but God says that Jesus is *also* the firstborn from the dead. Well, don't you know that if there's a first born there has to be a second born, a third born, a fourth born, a fifth born, and a sixth born? Thank God, I'm in that number somewhere. How about you?

Jesus is the firstborn. Let's look back over in John's Gospel, the very first chapter and read verse 14. This is a very interesting statement that John makes concerning Christ. You remember in verse 1 of the same chapter, he said, *"In the beginning was the Word, and the Word was with God, and the Word was God."* We now read in the 14th verse, *"And the Word was made flesh, and dwelt among us, (and we beheld his glory, the glory as of the only begotten of the Father, full of grace and truth."*

You see, at that time Jesus was the **only begotten**, but after He went to the cross and died and then arose from the dead and conquered death, He became the **firstborn** from the dead.

Jesus Actually Died Twice—

Whether you know it or not, Jesus had to die spiritually. Jesus died twice. The Bible says that Jesus became sin for us, and He condemned sin in the flesh. (See II Corinthians 5:21.) The only way that He could condemn sin in the flesh was to *become* sin. That's what He meant in the Garden of Gethsemane where Jesus was praying and He said, "Father, if it be thy will let this cup pass from me."

You ask, "What's He doing in the Garden with a cup?"

He was metaphorically speaking. That "cup" that He was talking about contained all the dregs of sin and damnation, and Jesus was about to drink that cup and become sin. His very nature, His very spirit consciousness rebelled against that, and He said, "Father, if there's any other way, let this cup pass from me," because it meant that **He who was spiritually alive** to God, and had not known sin, would **now die spiritually** by drinking that cup. That cup represented the sin of the entire world.

Jesus had to die spiritually. If He had not died spiritually, He couldn't have died physically.

If Jesus was going to be our sacrifice, He had to die and become sin. That's what it meant when it said, He became sin for us. He died spiritually. Then, when He was raised from the dead, He was born again spiritually, and He became the first begotten from the dead. God raised Him up and He was born again in the spirit.

You need to understand, Jesus was not sin in the natural. He did not come into the world as a sinner. He came into the world without the sin nature, but He had to **become** sin in order to condemn sin in the flesh. So He willingly offered himself up and died on behalf of man to redeem man.

When Adam died, he plunged the whole human race into sin. When Jesus died, He turned it around and brought us back to God. When God raised Him up, He became the *first begotten* from the dead. (Colossians 1:18.)

When Jesus told Nicodemus, "You must be born again," that's when we become number two, number three, etc.

You have to get that in your SPIRIT. You can't get it in your brain. That's what happened. The Bible said, **He who knew no sin became sin.**

How did Jesus become sin?

The only way He could become sin was to die in the spirit. When He died in the spirit, He condemned sin in the flesh and offered himself up as a living sacrifice; then when God raised Him from the dead, He became the firstborn from the dead. Jesus was actually born again. He was the first one to be born again.

Jesus willingly **became sin for us. He** had **a choice** and He offered himself up as a living sacrifice and condemned sin in the flesh.

Born Again By The Word And Spirit—

Now, we can be born again as a result of what Jesus did for us, and because of what He did for us, we can become legally the sons of God. First Peter 1:23 says the very same words that Jesus used when He talked to Nicodemus. *"Being born again, not of corruptible seed, but of incorruptible, by the word of God, which liveth and abideth for ever."* We are born again by the Word of God.

Jesus said, "Except a man be born of water and of the Spirit, he cannot enter into the kingdom of God" (John 3:5). The word *water* there is not **water baptism.** Many people are thinking that's what it means. But it is not water baptism. The word *water* is symbolic for the WORD. You are born again of the Word of God and the Spirit of God. It is the Spirit that quickeneth or makes us alive through the Word. As the Spirit of God impregnates or energizes that Word, it becomes alive within us.

There are two agents involved in the new birth just as there are two agents involved in natural birth.

It takes a male and a female; it takes a sperm and an egg. The sperm fertilizes the egg, conception takes place, and a child is born out of its mother's womb into the world.

The spiritual birth is on this wise: The Word of God goes forth. The Holy Spirit fertilizes that Word and it bursts into life within us, and a man is born out of the world into Christ Jesus.

You see, water baptism couldn't have a thing in the world to do with your salvation, because if it did then that would mean that you are saved by works. That would contradict Ephesians 2:8-9 which says, *"For by grace are ye saved through faith; and that not of yourselves: it is the gift of God: Not of works, lest any man should boast."*

If baptism is the way you get saved, then that would be a work, wouldn't it? That is something we do. God doesn't come down here and baptize anybody in water. God the Father doesn't baptize in water. I've never seen the Holy Ghost baptize anybody in water, and I've never seen Jesus baptize in water. No, men do that. It is a work, something that we do. It is something that we participate in. The Bible says that a man is born again and *saved without* works. It's grace; it's a gift of God. That word *water* stands for the Word of God.

All through the Scriptures there are words that are used as synonyms for the Word of God. "My Word is like a *hammer*, that breaks the rock in pieces" (Jeremiah 23:29). "Thy Word is a *lamp* unto my feet and a *light* to my path." Does that mean like an electric light? No. Does it mean that the Word is actually a hammer that you can take in your hand and break rocks with it? No! The word *water* then is emblematic, symbolic of God's WORD, there in the 3rd chapter of John. Peter is telling us that the incorruptible seed is THE WORD OF GOD.

The Spirit quickens the Word or makes the Word alive to you, and then you are born again, *out* of the world and *into* the family of God.

Remember we are talking about principle number three: **We must Know the Reality of the New Creation.** We have been born again, so we are new creatures in Christ Jesus. We are legally the sons of God. That means that we are heirs and joint-heirs with Christ. All of the glories of heaven belong to us because we are the living sons of God.

It is up to us to act like we are the sons of the living God. The reason that more of us don't have any more than we do is because we are not acting like we are the sons of God. We are acting like we are the sons of some poverty-stricken person that's out of a job.

Ephesians 2:1 tells us, *"And you hath he quickened,* (made alive) *who were dead in trespasses and sins."* You were dead! You were dead in sins; you were dead in trespasses. It says that He has quickened you or made you alive in Christ. *"Even when we were dead in sins, hath quickened us together with Christ, (by grace ye are saved;)"* (verse 5). Notice, "Even when you were dead in sins." The spiritual man **was** dead in sins, but that man has now been quickened or made alive in Jesus Christ.

Let's go on to verse 10: *"For we are his workmanship, created in Christ Jesus unto good works, which God hath before ordained that we should walk in them."*

Do you realize that every time you belittle yourself, every time you say "I'm unworthy, I'm no good, or I'm weak and I can't make it, and I'm not good enough," you are casting aspersions on God's fair creation? When you confess that you're weak and unworthy, that you can't make it, that you can't do it, that God won't hear your prayers, you are saying that God's fair creation is no good. We just read, *"For we are HIS workmanship."* We are the very workmanship of God, created in Christ Jesus! So, you are not unworthy. YOU ARE WORTHY. You're not unrighteous. YOU ARE RIGHTEOUS in Christ Jesus, or else God's fair creation isn't very good.

When you start seeing yourself like that, when you start looking at yourself and saying, "I'm a son of God! I'm a son of the King! I'm an heir and a joint-heir with Jesus Christ. I am worthy! I am righteous. I am a new creature in Christ Jesus," when you begin to say that instead of all the negativism you have been confessing, you will begin to rise up to that plateau where you'll be able to exercise strong faith.

Get Rid Of Your Sin Consciousness—

I used to condemn myself. I hear people who go to prayer meetings and get up and testify, "Well, I'm just an old sinner saved by grace." When they say that, they are still confessing that they are sinners.

I thought that, after you were saved, you were not a sinner any more. I **was** a sinner and thank God I **was** saved by grace, but **now I am a new creature in Christ.**

When you say you're a sinner saved by grace, you're still confessing that you're in the same state that you were in before Jesus saved you. No! I am not a sinner. You may be a sinner, but I am not a sinner saved by grace. I **was** a sinner and thank God, I **was saved** by grace, but **now I am a new creature in Christ Jesus.**

If you are a new creature then you are not what you used to be. So, stop confessing that garbage and thinking that you are being humble. When you do that, you are being ignorant and you are feeding the devil's lie. You are sapping off your own strength and vitality, spiritually speaking, by confessing something that you are not. You just read, *"We are his workmanship, created in Christ Jesus."*

Do you mean to tell me that God is in the business of creating sinners? If you are created in Christ Jesus and you're still an old sinner saved by grace, then you are saying that God created a sinner. It looks to me like He wasted His time because you already were a sinner. He didn't need to do anything. He could have saved that energy, isn't that right?

Stop saying that. You are not a sinner saved by grace. You used to be a sinner but thank God, God saved you by His grace, and now you are a new creation. You have been born again. You are a son of the King. You are a son of God.

If you *feel* like you're a sinner then you ought to stop *living* like a sinner. Then you won't feel like one. You have to remember that all of your past life is gone. It's dead; it's buried, it is done away with, praise God! It's already been judged and it will never rise against you in the day of judgment. You've been set free from it. Thank God, all that you used to be, you're not that now.

You need to stop telling yourself that you are a sinner saved by grace. You need to stop bringing up all of that garbage that you did ten years ago. If you are constantly confessing all of that stuff, that's being very stupid, because once God remits your sins they are remitted forever.

In Isaiah 43:25, God tells us this: *"I, even I, am he that blotteth out thy transgressions for mine own sake, and will not remember thy sins."* He blotted out your sins not for your sake, but for His own. If God doesn't remember it, why are you remembering it?

I used to do that. I would get in the prayer meeting and pray all that stuff and confess sins over and over. I thought I had to do that until I got in one of those "good moods." You know, I would confess until the tears started rolling down my cheeks and then I knew I'd reached the throne of God. I would have those tears coming down and burning my cheeks and I could pray. *I felt good*, like I was doing something. I *felt* like I had put it all together. Then, I would walk right out of the church and as soon as I stepped down the first step there was the devil with a hammer in his hand. "Whop," and I was down again.

I was building into myself sin consciousness. Every time I confessed what I had confessed before, I kept building into myself sin consciousness.

When you are born again there should be no more sin consciousness, because God said, *"I will blot out thy transgressions for mine own sake, and will not remember thy sins."*

When you sin, you should confess that sin and forget it. The devil will try to make you keep remembering it. If you think that you are being humble by remembering it, you are really being very foolish, because Satan is holding you in the bag; he's holding you in bondage.

The Bible says, *"If we confess our sins, he is faithful and just to forgive us our sins, and to cleanse us from all unrighteousness"* (I John 1:9).

Well, Reader, once you are forgiven, then it's over with. If you bought a car and you have made that 36th payment, the next year, you don't still sit around talking about it. You paid the thing off. You don't still say, "Oh, what am I going to do about the car payment? Oh, I'm going to have to pay!" No! that's over, so you forget it. You take the car and enjoy it now. You are foot-loose and fancy free as far as that car payment is concerned. You don't get your list of bills and include the car payment any more.

It is the same way with sin. God forgets about it, after you ask Him to forgive you. Oh that's beautiful! I'm glad He forgets it! There are some things that I have done that I sure wouldn't want to be remembered. I was freed when I read that verse. I said, "Praise God! If he doesn't remember, then I can forget it too, and I'm glad to forget it. Put it under the carpet and step on it. Put the chair over it so nobody can see the bump in the rug. Praise God."

Somebody says, "Well, you are just giving license to sinning now. You're just making it too easy."

I didn't make it easy. God did! I didn't say I would not remember your sins. God said that. If that's making it easy, then God's the one that's guilty, not Fred Price. Right? He's the one who said, "I'll forgive your sins and cleanse you from all unrighteousness." He is the one who said, "I'll remember your sins no more." If it's being made easy, God's the one who did it. No! We're not making it easy. We are finally getting it to you, the thing that belonged to you all the time. You just didn't know that it belonged to you!

That is not a license for sinning. Many of you are going to do enough sinning without a license. You don't need a license to sin.

Look at this: *"For by one offering he hath perfected for ever them that are sanctified.*

"Whereof the Holy Ghost also is a witness to us: for after that he had said before,

"This is the covenant that I will make with them after those days, saith the Lord, I will put my laws into their hearts, and in their minds will I write them;

"And their sins and iniquities will I remember no more.

"Now where remission of these is, there is no more offering for sin. Having therefore, brethren, boldness to enter into the holiest by the blood of Jesus.

"By a new and living way, which he hath consecrated for us, through the veil, that is to say, his flesh;

"And having an high priest over the house of God;

"Let us draw near with a true heart in full assurance of faith, having our hearts sprinkled from an evil conscience, and our bodies washed with pure water" (Hebrews 10:14-22).

Your conscience should be free from all of that past sin. Glory to God, it's beautiful to have a clear conscience. We ought to come with assurance, He says.

You don't have to come with your tail between your legs. You don't have to come bowing down, scraping and crawling on your hands and knees. It says, "Let us draw near with a true heart in full assurance."

When you have full assurance about something, you can walk boldly. You can walk tall. You don't have to hunch over when you are assured of something. God's Word is telling you right here, "with full assurance."

Now remember, we are talking about principle number three: **We Must Know the Reality of the New Creation.** Thank God, we are new creatures in Christ Jesus.

I don't know about you, but I am a new creature in Christ Jesus. He has made me NEW. It's exciting to be a new creature, to be able to put down that old way, that old life of the past, and throw it in the trash can and leave it. The devil would like to bring it out of the can and remind you of your past sins, but you have to stand against him and tell him, "Devil, you're a liar. The Bible told me to come with full assurance of faith."

In Romans 6:23 it says this, *"For the wages of sin is death; but the gift of God is eternal life through Jesus Christ our Lord."* Are you in Jesus Christ?

If you are in Christ, then you have passed from death into life.

Jesus tells us, *"Verily, verily, I say unto you, He that heareth my word, and believeth on him that sent me, hath everlasting life, and shall NOT come into condemnation; but is passed from death unto life"* (John 5:24).

If you are a new creature in Christ Jesus, you have passed from death unto life. The word *condemnation* means judgment. There is no more judgment for you concerning sin. You have been judged by the blood of Jesus and God has accepted you as His own son. You need to start living like it.

You are not weak and forlorn. You're not down at the bottom of the ladder or at the bottom of the barrel, crying, "Oh Lord, have mercy on me."

He has already had mercy on you. Gird up the loins of your mind, stand tall for you are a son of God. You are an heir to all that heaven has to offer. You don't have to back into anybody's door. You can walk in boldly because you have the mandate of heaven that all things are yours.

Now remember, Jesus said we've passed from death unto life. The Bible says that we're new creatures in Christ Jesus, we've been born again, not by corruptible, but by incorruptible seed. We are the children of God. And God doesn't remember our sins any more!

Let's look at another scripture that goes right along with what Jesus said. *"There is therefore now no condemnation to them which are in Christ Jesus, who walk not after the flesh, but after the Spirit"* (Romans 8:1).

There is no judgment for you. You'll never be judged to find out whether you're saved or lost. You are either saved now or you're lost now. My friend, you are either a child of God now or you are not a child of God. You need to get it together. You need to understand that you have been made free. You are a new creature in Christ Jesus. You need to start acting like it is true.

You're Legally Free—

Paul tells us, *"Knowing this, that our old man is crucified with him, that the body of sin might be destroyed, that henceforth we should not serve sin. For he that is dead is freed from sin"* (Romans 6:6-7).

The Bible says that we are free from sin, but we have to understand how he means this. Some of our brethren go around with the attitude, "Oh, I can't sin. I mean it's impossible for me to sin. I'm free of sin. I'm living free from sin."

That is not what he is saying. He's not saying that you CAN'T SIN. He's not saying that YOU'RE ABOVE SIN, but what he is saying is, YOU HAVE BEEN LEGALLY SET FREE FROM THE AUTHORITY AND THE BONDAGE OF SIN. You can still sin if you desire to sin. You can still serve sin if you want to serve sin.

I want to show you something in relationship to what we just read. We just read in that 7th verse of Romans 6, "For he that is dead is freed from sin." That means free from a legal standpoint. That means that sin does not have a legal right to hold you in bondage. It doesn't mean that you're outside the possibility of sinning. It doesn't mean that you're delivered into a world where there is no sin. It means that you don't **have** to sin, but you **can** if you choose to.

Jesus said, *". . . Verily, verily, I say unto you, Whosoever committeth sin is the servant of sin. And the servant abideth not in the house for ever: but the Son abideth ever. If the Son therefore shall make you free, ye shall be free indeed"* (John 8:34-36).

What Jesus is saying is, if you are a servant of sin then sin is your master. If you commit sin then you are serving your master (sin). In other words you are freed from that master, when Jesus said, "If the Son therefore shall make you free, ye shall be free indeed." He means that you're freed from that master. That master doesn't have any more legal jurisdiction over your life. You're set free, but that doesn't mean that the master isn't still there. It just means that you're free from any legal hold that he has on you and you don't have to serve him anymore. You fool yourself if you say he's not still there. Sin is still there and you can commit it anytime you get ready.

You need to understand that you have been set free, legally, from sin. It has no legal dominion over you. When temptation comes, you don't *have* to sin. You can say, "No, I refuse to do that, praise God. I've been set free from sin. I'm not the servant of sin and sin has no more jurisdiction or legal hold upon my life."

Many Christians think, "Well, I'm just doing what comes naturally. I just feel like it so I just do it. If God didn't want me to do it, I wouldn't feel like doing it."

That is a lie from the devil. If you believed it and sinned because you believed it, you wouldn't resist the sin. Satan put that thought in there to bring you into bondage.

Let's go back to Romans 6 again and read the 6th and 7th verses in the light of what Jesus said. *"Knowing this, that our old man is crucified with him, that the body of sin might be destroyed, that henceforth we should not serve sin."* Please notice, "That we SHOULD NOT SERVE SIN." It didn't say we **would** not, it said we **should** not. *"For he that is dead is freed from sin."* Meaning that **sin has no legal hold on you** anymore. Praise God, you are free!

That's just like if you have a contract and you bought that automobile and at the end of the 36 months, you paid that last payment and you have the pink slip. Six weeks later those rascals can't come knocking on your door and say, "You still owe us another payment."

You can say, "No sir, I have the pink slip, marked **paid in full**. It's my car. I've been set free from that contract."

If they can scare you into it, and get you to sign another contract, or piece of paper, then they legally have you in bondage again, and they can take you to court and make you pay.

All right, let's look at verse 11 of the same chapter. He says, *"Likewise reckon ye also yourselves to be dead indeed unto sin, but alive unto God through Jesus Christ our Lord."* When he said *reckon yourself,* the word *reckon* means count yourself as dead. In

other words it literally means "act like you're dead."
He is telling you to act like you are dead to sin.

We read this in verse 12, *"Let not sin therefore
reign in your mortal body, that ye should obey it in
the lusts thereof."* When he said *let it not reign,* that
means you **could** let it reign. He is telling us, *don't let
it reign,* meaning then that it can't reign unless you
allow it to reign. It can't be there unless you **will** it to
be there, unless you **desire** it to be there, because you
can do something about it.

We will read verse 13 of the same chapter.
*"Neither yield ye your members as instruments of
unrighteousness unto sin."* What are you doing with
your body? That means that you can keep from
yielding your body to sin, doesn't it? That means you
have authority. If the Bible tells you not to yield, that
means that you are capable of not yielding. Otherwise
God is unjust in requiring you to do something that
you are incapable of doing.

Verse 14 tells us, *"For sin shall not have dominion
over you: for ye are not under the law, but under
grace."* Thank God we are under grace and sin doesn't
have any dominion over us. But you have to act like it
is true. That's how it gets done. **You have to act like
you're free from sin.**

We read in verse 18, *"Being then made free from
sin, ye became the servants of righteousness."* You are
made free. God says you are free.

Somebody says, "Well, you know, you just have to pray every day because you know you have sinned some way."

That's a lie that the devil has planted in your mind to keep you sin conscious. You know when you sin, and if you don't think you've sinned, forget it.

You can count on this, if you don't have a sin consciousness or guilt consciousness, don't drum up one, because I'll guarantee you that whenever you sin the devil will be the first one to let you know about it. Many people try to work themselves into a feeling of condemnation so that they can confess something, and they ruin their faith.

Verse 22 of the same chapter says, *"But now being made free from sin, and become servants of God, ye have your fruit unto holiness, and the end everlasting life."* There it is again, "and being made free from sin." I didn't write it. We're FREE!

Paul tells us this, "Be ye not unequally yoked together with unbelievers: for what fellowship hath righteousness with unrighteousness? And what communion hath light with darkness?" (II Corinthians 6:14). You see, you are righteousness. You don't do anything to GET righteousness; you ARE righteousness and you ought to live righteously. You don't do good works to get righteous. When Paul said, "What communion hath light with darkness?", he is telling us that we are the light of the world. When Jesus was here He said, "I am the light of the world." And He told us to *let our light shine.* There is light in you.

Let's read on, verse 15, "And what concord hath Christ with Belial? or what part hath he that believeth with an infidel?" Belial stands for satanic things, or Satan or demons. We're Christ, He is the head and we are the body, so the head and the body are one and the same. The head is as much Christ as the body is; the body is as much Christ as the head.

He goes on to tell us in verse 16, "And what agreement hath the temple of God with idols? for ye are the temple of the living God; as God hath said, I will dwell in them, and walk in them; and I will be their God, and they shall be my people."

You are the people of God. You are the sons and daughters of God. You have been born again. You are a new creature in Christ Jesus. You have been set free from sin and its dominion. God has forgotten about your past sins. He doesn't remember them anymore.

Thank Him for His grace and walk on as a child of God. Take those things that God has made available to you through Christ's redemptive work on Calvary and begin to live the overcoming and victorious life.

THEN you will Know the Reality of the New Creation.

4

Know the Reality of Your Righteousness in Christ

There are many Christians who believe in God, who believe in Christ, who go to church very regularly, who would count it the "unpardonable sin" if they didn't go to church and wouldn't feel right the rest of the week; yet they have not learned how to exercise strong faith.

They pray every day, "Lord, give me more faith. Lord, give me more faith."

Some have even fasted for it. Some have even gone to prayer services and prayer groups. They have called on the telephone, sent telegrams, and everything else to get people to "pray for me that I'll have enough faith to make it through."

If you are in Christ, if you know Him as your personal Savior, YOU HAVE FAITH! If you say you don't have faith, you are calling God a liar.

The Bible tells us that we have faith. What is wrong is many of us have **faith** that is **weak.** That's why it won't operate.

When a battery is weak it won't start the car, and neither will weak faith start things rolling in your life, spiritually. You have to have STRONG FAITH if you want the best that God has to offer and the best that is available to you. God wants you to have the best, but it's secured and procured by or through the avenue of faith.

I am interested in strong faith and the Bible tells me that I can have it! When you begin to move in the arena of STRONG FAITH, things will begin to click for you in your spiritual life.

Many people believe God. Many people believe the Bible, and they say, "Oh yes, I believe the Bible. I believe it's the Word of God. I believe it from Genesis to Revelation." But, right then as they say that, they are preparing to go to the hospital the next week to be operated on.

The Bible says, *"With His stripes you were healed"* (I Peter 2:24). That means if you *were healed,* you *are healed.* If you are healed, that means you're not sick; and if you're not sick, you don't need an operation, do you? That's what the Bible says!

Others are saying, "Well, I don't know how I'm going to make ends meet. I'm having it so hard since the cost of living is going up. I just don't know what to do. Things are really tight now, how am I going to make it?"

They say that they believe the Bible from Genesis to Revelation.

Do they?

The Bible says, *"But my God shall supply all your need according to his riches in glory by Christ Jesus"* (Philippians 4:19).

You Have To Act On What You Believe—

It is more than just believing. You have to ACT on what you believe. You have to take what you believe and then do something about it. That's what faith is. **Faith is doing something about what you believe.**

If you say you believe and you are not doing it, you are fooling yourself. If you say you believe God's Word — that you believe the Bible, and believe God — but you're still whipped with sickness and disease; you're still under the poverty syndrome and don't have enough to make ends meet, then something is wrong, friend — something is radically wrong!

Many people come to me and say, "Oh I have great faith, Pastor, I've always believed," and right then they are frustrated, and they don't know which way to go.

If you have faith use it. EXERCISE IT.

Thus far through these printed pages, we have discussed the following principles:

Principle number one: **You must Know the Reality of the Word of God.**

Principle number two: **You must Know the Reality of your Redemption in Christ.**

Principle number three: **You must Know the Reality of the New Creation,** that we are new creatures in Christ Jesus.

And now we are going to discuss principle number four: You must **Know the Reality of your Righteousness in Christ.**

You will never be a successful Christian until you know all of these things that we have discussed — not think them, not hope them, but KNOW THEM AS A REALITY, as a vital part of your everyday life. Until then, you will be a beggar in spiritual matters.

Become The Master Of Your Circumstances—

When you realize these principles and make them a part of your life, you will begin to ACT like what the Bible says is true, and begin to DO what the Bible says to do. Then YOU WILL POSSESS STRONG FAITH. When you learn to do this, you will not become a *victim* of circumstances, but you will become the *master* of circumstances.

Now, I am not talking about the **Power of Positive Thinking.** I'm not talking about **Science of the Mind, Mind Science,** or **Christian Science.** I'm not talking about the **Science of Living.** I am talking about FAITH IN THE WORD OF THE LIVING GOD.

All of these other things that I mentioned use some of the terminology that the Bible uses, but they are not using it in the context in which the Bible is giving it. They do get some results, but those results are minimal. They are only temporary results.

I am interested in the long-term investment myself. I'm interested in that investment that carries me on through the gates of glory, to the very presence of God where I can stand before His throne and talk to Him, face to face.

Do you just want the things of this world and this life? When you reach the end, do you just want to be put in the ground while a preacher stands over you and says, "The Lord giveth and the Lord taketh away; blessed be the name of the Lord. He came into the world naked. He brought nothing in, and he's taking nothing out; earth to earth, dust to dust, and ashes to ashes"? If that is all you are interested in, you can have it!

But you can have all those other things that I have mentioned before, right now! You don't have to wait until you get to heaven. The things I am talking about are WHAT CHRIST SAID THAT HE CAME TO GIVE US.

He said He came that we might have life and have it more abundantly (John 10:10b), not just **pie-in-the-sky, by-and-by**. Thank God for the pie-in-the-sky, but He wants you to have ice cream, cookies, cake, and soda pop right now in this life! You can have it all. God wants you to have it, but there are some principles by which you must receive it. If you are not receiving by the principles that God has laid down, then you are not getting it from God the Father.

Remember, all that glitters is not gold.

We read in Romans chapter 3, beginning with verse 20, "Therefore by the deeds of the law there shall no flesh be justified (literally, **declared righteous**) in his sight: for by the law is the knowledge of sin.

"But now the righteousness of God without the law is manifested, being witnessed by the law and the prophets;

"Even the righteousness of God which is by faith of Jesus Christ unto all and upon all them that believe: for there is no difference:

"For all have sinned, and come short of the glory of God;

"Being justified (declared righteous) freely by his grace through the redemption that is in Christ Jesus:

"Whom God hath set forth to be a propitiation through faith in his blood, to declare his righteousness for the remission of sins that are past, through the forbearance of God;

"To declare, I say, at this time his righteousness: that he might be just, and the justifier of him which believeth in Jesus" (Romans 3:20-26).

In the last verse, the words *just* and *justifier* in the Greek are rendered this way: "To declare, I say, at this time his righteousness: that he might be righteous, even when declaring righteous, him which believeth in Jesus."

"Even when declaring righteous, them that believe in Jesus." From this passage of Scripture, we can see from God's standpoint that righteousness is not an attainable goal that you can get by your works.

Many people have used this Scripture passage down through the years to try to get people to do things, so they could get righteous. But in the economy of God there is nothing that you can do to be righteous. Thank God there is nothing that you **have** to do to be righteous.

If you lived ten million years and did ten million good works, you would never be righteous in God's sight, because you can't obtain righteousness by your own efforts. That's where many Christians are deceived by the devil.

Some Christians think that going to church makes them righteous. Some think that doing good deeds makes them righteous. Some Christians think that selling chicken dinners and having barbecue dinners on Saturday afternoons to raise money to support God's program makes them righteous. Some think that having women's day and men's day programs to raise money and finances is being righteous.

None of that can make you righteous. None of that — not one single work that you can ever do will make you righteous.

Thank God! We are righteous because we are IN Jesus Christ. God counts us as righteous because Jesus is righteous.

Righteousness Is A Gift—

It is a gift. You can't earn it. You can't work for it. You can't do any good works to get it. **You have to**

be accounted and declared righteous by God. When He declares you righteous, you are righteous!

Righteousness is not something that you *do*. *IT'S SOMETHING THAT GOD DOES FOR YOU.* You are righteous if you are a Christian and you are as righteous as you are ever going to get.

I used to think that I had to do things to get righteous, and then when I didn't do those things, when I failed in doing them, I felt unrighteous. I didn't understand that the Bible says that God has declared us righteous.

I'm not teaching you some denominational doctrine, I'm not giving you what this church believes, or what that church believes. I am giving you what the Bible says about righteousness.

In America, we use linear measurements — inches, feet, yards, etc. Now, you can say, "Well, I think that is an inch," or "That seems to me to be about a foot long."

It doesn't matter what you think a foot is. If what you think to be a foot does not conform to twelve inches on the ruler, it is not a foot. It is not what you think about how long a foot is, it's what the ruler has to say.

Here God's Word is the ruler. It is what God says, not what you think, not what your denomination says, not what my denomination says, not what I say; it is only so because God says it is so.

In Romans we have this statement, *"For if by one man's offence death reigned by one; much more they which receive abundance of grace and of the gift of righteousness shall reign in life by one, Jesus Christ"* (Romans 5:17). To reign is the term that you use concerning a king who is sitting on a throne and ruling a kingdom. The word *reign* literally means to rule. "For if by one man's offence (that one man was Adam), death ruled by one; much more they which receive abundance of grace and of the GIFT OF RIGHT-EOUSNESS shall reign (rule) in life by one, Jesus Christ." Not rule in heaven, not rule in the sweet by-and-by, not rule when you die, but "reign in life." That means *now* in *this* life. The *Amplified New Testament* says, "shall reign as kings in life." That means in this life. In this life you are to rule.

Rule what?

You are to rule your circumstances. You are to rule your environment. You should exert an influence on things around you. Jesus did. The Old Testament saints did. Elijah and Elisha did.

When Elijah wanted to cross the Jordan River and there were no bridges or ferries to take him across, he took his mantle from around his neck and slapped the water with it. Everywhere he slapped the water, dry land appeared. As the water went back, he stepped on that; then he slapped another place and stepped on that, as he walked across on dry land.

Elijah also changed the circumstances. By praying one time, it didn't rain for three-and-one-half years. He ruled the circumstances.

Jesus stopped a storm one time. He told the sea to be still and the waves to lie down — and they did! He said of the believer, "The works that I do shall he do also; and greater works than these shall he do because I go unto my Father" (John 14:12).

You, as a Christian, are supposed to be the master of your circumstances.

I know you have been taught that the circumstances were supposed to master you, that they were God's will for you, but this verse doesn't say that. There is no way in the world you can reign as a king in life and be poor, or reign as a king in life and be poverty-stricken.

Some people have decided not to follow the Christian way because of the false image that has been portrayed over the years. "If you are a Christian and if you really believe in Jesus, you won't have anything in this life."

So, some have said, "Man, I ain't had nothing all my life and I'm not about to stop now. I'm gonna get all I can get as fast as I can, any way I can." They have turned from the Gospel because of this poverty picture that the church has presented to the world for so long.

Notice again, he said in Romans 5:17, *"For if by one man's offence death reigned* (ruled) *by one; much more they which receive abundance of grace and of the gift of righteousness shall reign in life by one Jesus Christ."*

Notice the last part of that verse, **"gift of righteousness."** GIFT!

What is a gift?

A gift is something that one person gives to another person, and he gives it because he wants to give it. You couldn't pay him for it. If you did, it would cease to be a gift. It would become a wage. But when you give it to a person FREELY, because you want to, that is a gift. There's nothing you can do but receive it or reject it.

Righteousness is a gift from God. You don't have to do anything to **get** righteousness except **receive** it. When you receive Jesus Christ as your personal Savior, God, right at that moment, gives to you the gift of righteousness.

"Therefore, as by the offence of one judgment came upon all men to condemnation; even so by the righteousness of one the **free gift** *came upon all men unto justification of life"* (verse 18). The word *condemnation* means judgment. He is telling us that by the righteousness of Jesus Christ, the free gift came upon all men unto justification of life, or unto the declaration of them being righteous.

"For as by one man's disobedience many were made sinners, so by the obedience of one shall many be made righteous" (verse 19). Notice, they **will be made righteous.** They **won't earn** righteousness; they **won't work** until they arrive at it. He said **by the obedience of one,** meaning Christ, THEY SHALL BE MADE RIGHTEOUS.

God Makes You Righteous—

I thank God today that I am righteous. If I said that I'm not righteous, I would be saying that God's Word is untrue, because the BOOK just said, "that many shall be made righteous."

"Moreover the law entered, that the offence might abound. But where sin abounded, grace did much more abound. That as sin hath reigned unto death, even so might grace reign (rule) *through righteousness unto eternal life by Jesus Christ our Lord"* (verses 20-21).

Now we need to understand, if we are Christians, we ARE righteous.

What does righteousness mean literally? What does the Bible mean when it says **righteousness**?

You see, we have a lot of words that we use in what we call a "religious context." When we do this, they become very mysterious to us. They almost become untouchable to us because we don't understand what they mean.

We get over here in a religious bag, as it were, which is entirely false and make believe or a fairy tale. We look at these words, "righteousness, justification, and grace," and we don't quite know what they mean.

Let's look at the word *grace*. If you were to walk over to the insurance office and ask a man, "What does *grace* mean?" he would tell you that it means unmerited favor. After the premium on your insurance policy becomes due, the company gives you a "grace period." You can go so long without making any payments and you're still covered by the insurance policy. In other words, it's something that you don't deserve. It is something that you haven't earned. It's something that the company does for you. It's unmerited favor and it means something that you don't have to do anything to get, but just receive it.

Ask the average Christian, "What does *grace* mean?"

He starts trying to figure out what the word means. He starts thinking about the song, "Amazing Grace," and he says, "Ah, grace, ah, it means, well, ah, I really don't know."

Did you know that the word GRACE means the very same thing that it meant in the insurance office? It means unmerited favor. It means somebody is giving you something that you don't deserve and they don't *have* to give it to you. All you have to do is receive it. Grace is something given to you that you haven't earned.

Now let's look at the word *righteousness*. What does the word *righteousness* mean literally?

Righteousness means **right standing with God.** That's simply what it means. It means you are right with God. Righteousness means you have a right standing with God. It means that you stand on an equality with God. You have an authority and a right to stand before God and talk to Him just like you would talk to you own earthly father.

To be righteous, then, means that God has declared us on an equality with himself. We can go to Him and talk to Him anytime we get ready. We can go to Him and expect Him to hear us. We can go to Him and expect Him to give us the things that we ask Him for, because we are right with God.

Some people think that being right with God is when everything they do is right and they haven't made any mistakes. The minute they make a mistake they say, "I'm not right with God anymore. I don't know what's going to happen to me."

When you make a mistake you are just as right with God as you were before you made that mistake, because what you do can't change your right standing with God. **You are born into that right standing through Jesus Christ.** All you have to do is to stand there and enjoy it!

You are right if you're in Jesus Christ.

On the other hand, if you are not in Christ then you're not right. You are unrighteous. You are not in right standing with God if you haven't been born again. But, **if you are a Christian, then you are right with God.**

Because that is true (you're born again), you have to act like you are righteous.

Sometimes the devil condemns you through your sins, and as most other people do, you probably don't *feel* righteous. When you don't feel very righteous you will let oppression come upon you. You will get to the point where your back is up against the wall and you can't motivate for yourself. It will look like every door is closed in your face. You will call your pastor and say, "Pastor, pray for me."

What you need to do is pray for yourself. You don't ask the pastor to put your shoes on for you, do you? You don't ask the pastor to bathe you, do you? No. The reason you do this is because you have allowed the devil to condemn you because of your sins, and you don't think that you are righteous. You don't think that God is going to hear you. The devil tells you that there's no point in your praying, because you aren't very righteous.

You'll believe the devil, yet you **say** you believe the Bible from Genesis to Revelation. You (when you do this) are believing the devil more than you are believing God. You are believing that lie that the devil places in your mind about your not being very righteous.

The Bible just told us that righteousness is a gift that God has given us.

You are righteous, and based upon the FACT that YOU ARE RIGHTEOUS, you ought to live that way. If you *live* that way you will *feel* righteous. If you don't feel very righteous, it's probably because you're not living it.

I feel righteous myself; not that I walk by feelings. I welcome feelings, but I don't base my faith on feelings. I base my faith on God's Word. I am as righteous as I am ever going to get because God gave righteousness to me. I didn't have to do anything but accept it, and I accepted it, praise God! I accepted it and He counts me righteous.

Based on that, I go forward, and I know that He hears me when I pray. I don't have to ask anybody to pray for me. I can, but I can pray for myself. It is true that **we should pray for one another,** but that's not a *need* that we have. It is a *privilege* that we are given.

My Father told me that I am righteous. He told me that I am in right standing with Him. He told me to ask and I will receive. He told me to seek and I will find; knock and He will open the door. (Matthew 7:7; Luke 11:9.)

If I don't believe that, then I am doubting my own Father. I need to act like it's true. I just ACT like the Bible is true, because it is true, and I go to Him and pray. I believe that He is going to hear me, because He told me that He would. Then, when I leave my prayer closet, I say, "Praise the Lord. I thank You Father that You have heard me, and I know I have what I have asked for." I go right on and act like it's so. I'm not doing it because I am super-spiritual. I am not doing it because I'm the pastor of a church. I am doing it because He told me that **He gave me the gift of righteousness,** and that means I am in right standing with Him. Therefore, all I need to do is just act like it's true and I get the blessings from Him.

You can keep depending on somebody else, waiting on them, and calling on them and waiting all hours of the night — waiting on them to get home so you can ask them to pray for you. While you are waiting on them to come home, you could die. The devil will kill you if he gets half a chance. What I am saying is, you can wait around for your pastor to get back in town to pray for you, but you don't have to. You have right standing with God. Your pastor doesn't have any more right standing than you do. The Bible said righteousness is a gift, and He gives it to everybody who receives Jesus Christ. If you have received Jesus Christ as your Savior, you have right standing with God. Use it!

In the natural world, sometimes you run into a person and you become very friendly with him. Later you find out that he has a very plush position, at a certain place. So, when things get out of line, and you must have something done, you will go to your friend because your friend is right there on the top level. You do it because you have that relationship with him.

You ask, "Will you do something for me?" and he will do it.

God is in the highest position of all: He is not the chairman of the board; He *is* the board. He's the conference room, the conference table, and all the delegates! He has all the voting stock. He's the whole company, and the Bible says that you have right standing with God.

When you need something done, you don't have to go to City Hall and go into the Mayor's office to see if he'll do something for you. You can go to the grand architect of the universe and say, "Father, I need something."

He will say, "It's yours. Just believe that you receive it and it's yours."

You will receive because God has made you righteous. As I said before, many condemn themselves because they don't *feel* very righteous. They think they won't be heard, so they go find somebody who they think is righteous, to pray for them.

According to the Bible, not according to denominational doctrine, not according to opinion, but according to the Bible, you have been given the gift of righteousness, if you are a child of God.

Come Boldly To The Throne Of Grace—

I didn't say that you are perfect. I said you are righteous; you have right standing with God. That means you can approach God and you don't have to bow your head and crawl in on your hands and knees, or back in through the door. You can walk right up to the throne because the Bible says you can.

The Bible tells us that we can come boldly to the throne of grace and find grace to help in time of need. That's our authority, that's our privilege because we are in Christ.

If you are a Christian, God has given you the gift of righteousness and you have been declared righteous by God.

Let's look at something else that the Bible says is of utmost importance to us: *"Confess your faults one to another, and pray one for another, that ye may be healed. The effectual fervent prayer of a righteous man availeth much"* (James 5:16).

Perhaps you read this scripture before and so you ran to get Kathryn Kuhlman (who is now with the Lord) to pray for you, or you ran to get Billy Graham to pray for you, or you have tried to find Oral Roberts so he could pray for you. You may have found some other preacher, or perhaps your own pastor to pray for you. You have read that and said, "Oh my, my, my, if only I were righteous. If only I were righteous, I could pray the effectual fervent prayer, but because I am not righteous, I can't pray it. I have to find somebody to pray it for me."

The Bible says that YOU have been given the gift of righteousness. YOU ARE RIGHTEOUS! When this verse talks about the effectual fervent prayer of a righteous man, God is talking about YOU. What God is saying is that YOUR effectual fervent prayer will avail MUCH, not a little, but much.

Get A Righteousness Consciousness—

You need to get a righteousness consciousness. Most of us have an **unrighteousness consciousness.** That is why we are defeated in our lives. That's why our prayers are not very real. That's why the Bible is not very real when we try to read it. That's why the church is not very real to us, because we have such a low estimate of ourselves. We do not see ourselves as

God sees us. We see ourselves as the devil has told us we are. We believe Satan's lie rather than believe God's Word.

We think we're being humble when we get up in a prayer service to give our testimony, and say, "Well, I'm just an old sinner saved by grace. You all pray for me that I'll have enough strength to make it through. I'm gonna hold on, I'm not going to give up, but you pray for me that I'll have enough strength to pray through and hold on."

That is not a prayer of faith. That is really stupidity, it is being ignorant of God's Word. If you say that, you don't know who YOU ARE IN CHRIST JESUS.

I am righteous because He has made me righteous, and based upon His righteousness I am more than a conqueror. I don't have to bow and scrape to Satan or any of his demons. I don't have to bow to circumstances. I change circumstances to fit my needs. That is Bible. That is the way it is.

We are righteous because He has made us that way. *"Therefore if any man be in Christ, he is a new creature: old things are passed away; behold, all things are become new.*

"And all things are of God, who hath reconciled us to himself by Jesus Christ, and hath given to us the ministry of reconciliation;

"To wit, that God was in Christ, reconciling the world unto himself, not imputing their prespasses unto

them; and hath committed unto us the word of reconciliation.

"Now then we are ambassadors for Christ, as though God did beseech you by us: we pray you in Christ's stead, be ye reconciled to God.

"For he hath made him to be sin for us, who knew no sin; that we might be made the righteousness of God in him" (II Corinthians 5:17-21). Not that we might work for it, not that we might earn it, but that we might be made the righteousness of God in Christ Jesus.

Praise God YOU are righteous. You may not believe it, but if you do not believe it, then you do not believe God's Word. YOU ARE RIGHTEOUS! Now, based upon that, if you ever actually get a right estimate of yourself, it will help you in a way that is very beautiful. It will make it very easy for you to live without sinning, because when you realize that you are righteous, you will say, "Well, I can't do that, I'm righteous."

The reason it is very easy for some of you to sin and keep on doing your dirt and garbage is because you don't know who you are. You just think that you are an old sinner, saved by grace; that you are weak and low; that it is inevitable that you are going to sin, so you might as well just go ahead and do it anyhow.

That is the devil's lie to keep you in bondage.

Declare Who You Are—

If you realize who you are you will say, "I can't do that. No, no, I am righteousness! I have been made a new creature in Christ Jesus! God lives in me! I can't do that." It will make it easy for you to reject temptations when they come.

"There hath no temptation taken you but such as is common to man, but God is faithful who will not suffer (allow) you to be tempted above that you are able; but will with the temptation also make a way to escape, that you may be able to bear it" (I Corinthians 10:13). God made a way of escape.

Do you know how you escape? By declaring who you are.

You escape by declaring in the face of the devil, and in the face of demons, who you are. You say, "Devil, take your hands off me, off my wife, my children, my home, my job, and everything I own because I am righteousness in Christ Jesus. I have been made righteousness. I am a new creature in Christ Jesus, and you have no legal right; you have no legal authority over my life. I resist you in the name of Jesus." When you do this, the demons and the devil will leave you alone!

Most people say, "Well, I'm just an old sinner saved by grace so I'll just go on and do this, and then I'll just come on to prayer meeting and get the folks to pray for me and then the Lord will forgive me."

Don't do that!

You declare in the face of sin the fact that you've been redeemed.

You declare in the face of poverty that Christ has redeemed you from the curse of the law.

You declare in the face of disease and sickness that would come walking and sniffing around your door, that with His stripes you are healed.

You say, "I don't have to receive what the devil is putting out. I don't have to take it, and I refuse to take it. I'm against poverty, and I'm against disease, and I refuse to be sick. I don't have to be sick; the Bible tells me that I'm righteousness. I've been made the righteousness of God in Christ Jesus, and my Bible tells me that He took my infirmities, He bore my sickness and with His stripes I was healed. The Bible says that He who was rich became poor that I through His poverty might become rich, so I refuse to be poor. I don't have to be poor!"

Become God-Inside-Minded—

You know what you need to do, friend, is become God-inside-minded. You need to learn how to think the thoughts of God — after Him. You need to look in the mirror of the Word and find out what God says about you. Then you need to believe that's who you are; begin to talk like that's who you are; begin to act like that's who you are. Begin to expect that the things you are will become manifested in your life, and they will!

As long as you go around with a low estimate of yourself, you won't make it. When you say that you won't make it, you rob yourself.

Thank God, you can confess what the Bible says about you. "For what fellowship hath righteousness with unrighteousness?" Righteousness is the believer, because the believer has been made righteous in Christ Jesus.

It matters not what you think about righteousness. You don't have to think that you are righteous. It doesn't matter whether you think I am righteous or not. I am righteous because my Father told me I am righteous. I am only concerned about what God says. He is the one who purchased my redemption. He is the one who made me a new creature in Christ Jesus. He holds the whole world in the hollow of His hands. I am only concerned about what He thinks.

If you are a Christian, you are made righteous through Jesus Christ. It shouldn't matter what someone else thinks. It shouldn't make any difference to you what someone else says. What should matter to you is what God's Word says about you, and He says that if you're born again, you are a new creature in Christ Jesus; that you are righteous.

The Bible says that when a man's ways please the Lord, He will make even his enemies to be at peace with him. (Proverbs 16:7.) Glory to God, that's what I am banking on!

The Power Of Positive Confession—

I'm banking on what my Father says about me, not even what I think about me. What I do is say what my Father says about me. I'm righteous! I am righteous! That's what you call the "power of positive confession."

After I say what my Father says about me, I begin to feel like I'm righteous. I didn't say perfect. I didn't say flawless. I said, "I am righteous." In other words I have a right standing with my Father. I can go to Him any time I want to, and I can get exactly what I want from Him.

Yes, that's what He told me. *"If ye abide in me, and my words abide in you, ye shall ask what ye will, and it shall be done unto you"* (John 15:7).

Please remember, YOU ARE RIGHTEOUS! Let's look at James 5:16 again, "Confess your faults one to another, and pray one for another, that ye may be healed. The effectual fervent prayer of a righteous man availeth much."

We say, "Well, that's beautiful and that's wonderful. I wish I were that righteous so my prayers could be heard, so I could pray effectually and fervently."

Let's continue on and read the 17th verse. *"Elias was a man subject to like passions as we are, and he prayed earnestly that it might not rain: and it rained not on the earth by the space of three years and six months."*

This is talking about Elijah, and it says that Elijah was a man of like passions as we are. Elijah is used as an illustration of a righteous man. You remember the great and mighty things Elijah did.

He smote the Jordan with his mantle and the waters parted. He stood on Mt. Carmel and challenged the 450 prophets of Baal and the 400 prophets of the Groves. Elijah stood there by himself and defeated every single one of them (850 false prophets) in the power of God. When Ahab left Mt. Carmel and got in his chariot and drove down through the plains of Jezreel to tell his wife, Jezebel, what had happened. Elijah took the border of his robe, tucked it into his girdle, and started running. He ran fourteen miles across the plains of Jezreel, outrunning a horse and chariot. You talk about moving, that man outran the chariot! The power of God was on him. He was a mighty man.

We read all about those great things that he did, and we say, "There's no way in the world that I could be like Elijah. There's no point in my even classifying myself with Elijah!"

God does! He classifies you with Elijah. God is the one who put those words in the Bible. He said, "The effectual fervent prayer of a righteous man availeth much," and then He gave us Elijah as an illustration of a righteous man.

But let's look at the other side of the ledger. There is something else about Elijah. Not only did Elijah outrun the chariot, but when he came into the city the news was out (*newspapers were out on the streets!*). Ahab had come back and told Jezebel, and she made the statement (*front page news!*) that she would "have Elijah's head by sundown."

She was the kind of woman who would do what she said. She had had many men killed. It didn't make any difference to her, she would have their heads cut off in a minute. One time, her weak and spineless husband, Ahab (he was the king), looked out of his window and saw a man next door (Naboth). Naboth had a beautiful vineyard. Ahab wanted that vineyard. He went down to talk to Naboth about it, and Naboth said, "No, we have had this vineyard in our family ever since I can remember. My grandfather worked in this vineyard. We have had this vineyard in our family for so long. I don't want to give it up."

Ahab, the king, went back into his chamber and lay down on the bed and cried. Yes — shed tears. Jezebel came in and said, "Man, what's the matter with you? Why are you crying?"

Ahab said, "I want Naboth's vineyard and he won't give it to be, bah, bah, bah!"

Jezebel said, "What's the matter with you? I'll get it for you!" She got it! She had the man killed, took the vineyard and gave it to her husband.

That's the kind of woman Jezebel was, and Elijah knew about her reputation. When he heard that she said she would have his head by sundown, Elijah started running again. This time he went out into the desert and the Spirit of the Lord was not upon him this time. He soon got tired and fell out, under a juniper tree. Finally he hid in a cave. The lightning came, and the earthquake came, the fire came, and God was not in any of these. Then — a still small voice spoke to Elijah. It was God. God said, "What are you doing out here?"

"Ah, ah, ah, haven't You heard? (*Haven't You read the evening paper?*) Jezebel is after me. I am trying to get away from that woman!"

This is the same man that the Bible uses as a man that is called "righteous!" He is running from a woman, but the Bible uses him as an illustration of a righteous man.

God asked, "What are you doing out here?"

Elijah said, "Lord, You might as well kill me. You might as well end my misery now, because I'm the only one left. There's not another person in Israel who is following after You but me. I'm the only one and You might as well kill me because she's going to get to me and kill me for sure. You might as well kill me."

God said, "I have seven thousand knees that haven't bowed to Baal. Get yourself together and get back into town and I will tell you what to do."

Here was Elijah, who had just single-handedly defeated 850 pagan prophets, running from one woman; but the Bible says that he was a righteous man. Why was he righteous? He wasn't righteous because he was running. He wasn't righteous because he whipped those prophets on the mountain. He was righteous because God accounted it to him for righteousness; because he dared to believe God. The Bible says he was a righteous man.

Friend, if Elijah's prayer was heard, your prayer will be heard, if you will dare to believe God. Elijah prayed and it didn't rain for three-and-one-half years. The Bible says, "The effectual fervent prayer of a righteous man availeth much."

You need to keep or maintain your righteousness consciousness. That is what's wrong with most people. They don't *feel* righteous. Because they don't feel righteous, they don't dare pray because they don't think that God is going to hear them.

Confess Your Sins—

One reason that you don't feel righteous is because you haven't confessed your sins. You may still have all those debts of sin hanging over your head. All you have to do is confess them and they are done away with. I John 1:9 tells us, *"If we confess our sins, he is faithful and just to forgive us our sins, and to cleanse us from all unrighteousness."*

Well, what does that word *unrighteousness* mean? It is the word *righteous* with a prefix *un*, which means *non-righteous*. So, the Bible says that if we confess our sins, He is faithful and just to forgive us our sins, and to cleanse us from all non-righteousness.

It is sin that keeps you from sensing in yourself or feeling that you are righteous. But the Bible says if you confess your sins, He will forgive you of those sins, and cleanse you from all unrighteousness.

It is somewhat like this:

A mother and daughter are in the kitchen. Mother has just baked a pan of cookies. The daughter asks the mother for some of them, but the mother says, "No, it's too close to dinner time."

A little later mother is in the bedroom and she hears what sounds like the lid on the cookie jar. As she walks into the kitchen, she sees her daughter atop the step stool with her hand in the cookie jar.

In a somewhat harsh tone mother says, "I thought I told you you couldn't have any cookies yet!"

The little girl bursts into tears and runs to her room.

What has happened? Fellowship has been broken. The relationship hasn't changed, but the *sense* of parent-child relationship has been broken because of this incident (sin). Regardless of how mother or daughter feel, they are still mother and daughter; but the child has lost her *sense* of righteousness (right standing).

A little later the child comes into the kitchen, puts her arms around her mother's waist, and says, "Mommy, I'm sorry. Please forgive me."

Mother says, "That's all right, sweetheart, I love you!" Now their fellowship is restored and the child's sense of righteousness (right standing) is restored. That's what happens when we sin.

All you have to do is just confess it. Tell God that you have sinned. Tell Him what you have done, and then forget it. Put it on Him, and He will wipe it away.

"My little children these things write I unto you, that ye sin not. And if any man sin, we have an advocate with the Father, Jesus Christ the righteous" (I John 2:1).

The ideal is: **don't sin**. When you **don't sin**, you will never lose your sense of righteousness consciousness.

God says, "don't sin," but praise God for His mercy. The next part of the verse tells us if we do sin, "we have an advocate with the Father, Jesus Christ the righteous." An advocate is somebody who stands in your stead, like a lawyer who pleads your case.

If you sin, just go to Him and say, "Father, I'm sorry. I've sinned. Forgive me." As soon as you say that, He has forgiven you.

Remember then, principle number four is:**You must Know the Reality of your Righteousness in Christ.**

5

Know the Reality of the Indwelling Spirit

As we continue our study on **How To Obtain Strong Faith — Six Principles,** we are ready to discuss principle number five: **You must Know the Reality of the Indwelling Spirit.**

Before we discuss this important principle, let's take a quick look at the first four principles that we have been studying.

Principle number one: **You must Know the Reality of God's Word.** God's Word is Spirit; it is life. You must get into the Word; continue in the Word; digest it and get it down into your spirit.

Principle number two: **You must Know the Reality of your Redemption in Christ.** You have been redeemed from the powers of darkness and from demonic authority.

Principle number three: **You must Know the Reality of the New Creation.** As a Christian, being born by the Spirit of God, you are a new creature in Christ Jesus. God views you as a brand new individual.

Principle number four: **You must Know the Reality of your Righteousness in Christ.** You must know that you are righteous in Christ. You don't have to do anything to get righteous. You are righteous in

Christ. Righteousness is a gift that is given to you when you receive Christ as your personal Savior. Consequently by knowing that, you ought to start living righteously and then you will start feeling righteous.

Now, we come to principle number five: **You must Know the Reality of the Indwelling Spirit.**

Please understand, when we talk about this principle, we are talking about those who have been filled with the Spirit.

You see, every Christian **is born of** the Spirit, but not every Christian **is filled with** the Spirit. To be filled with the Holy Spirit doesn't save you. You do have to be saved to be filled with the Holy Spirit, but you can be saved, born again, and not filled with the Holy Spirit. To be filled with the Holy Spirit is to give you supernatural power in your life.

Some denominations will try to tell you, "Honey, if you're not filled with the Holy Ghost and speaking in tongues, you are not even saved." That's not in the Bible. They don't know what they are talking about. It may be in their church denominational doctrine, but it is not in the Bible.

All Christians Are Not Filled With The Spirit—

You don't *have* to be filled with the Holy Ghost and speak with other tongues in order to be saved, but if you are saved you *can* be filled with the Holy Ghost and speak with other tongues. If you are a Christian you ought to be doing that, because God has made it available to you. If He made it available to you, He must want you to have it. If you aren't filled with the Holy Ghost, apparently you're not complete, because if you were complete you wouldn't need it.

When I say, **You must know the Reality of the Indwelling Spirit**, I am talking to those who have been filled with the Spirit. There are many who have been filled with the Spirit, who have had the experience of receiving the gift of the Holy Spirit, but they doubt it. They are not walking in the fullness of that power. They are not walking in the glory and in the "supernaturalness" of what God has done for them.

Some of you who read this book are still questioning; you're still crying and begging God. You are still trying to find something out there to give you power and to make your life more beneficial and more victorious. What you don't understand is that the Holy Ghost is inside you — not out there, but in you.

Until you know that as a living reality, then you will never be able to exercise strong faith.

We read in I John 4:4, *"Ye are of God, little children, and have overcome them: because greater is he that is in you, than he that is in the world."* The one that is in you or can be in you is the Holy Spirit. The one that is in the world is Satan. The Bible is telling you that He (the Holy Spirit) that's in you is greater than he (Satan) that is in the world.

So, the Holy Spirit in you is more powerful and stronger than Satan who is in the world.

You must realize that these letters are written to Spirit-filled believers. They are not written to nominal Christians. They are not written to those who have not yet received the gift of the Spirit. They are written to those who HAVE RECEIVED THE GIFT OF THE HOLY GHOST, and the Spirit of God is reminding them of what they have.

The Word says, **"Greater is he that is in you, than he that is in the world."** That's the reason that I cannot be defeated. That's the reason that I will not accept defeat; that's the reason that I will always walk on the top of the mountains and not under the mountains. The Bible told me that "greater is He that is in me than he that is in the world." I believe that and I act like it is so. Then, that power that God has given me begins to manifest itself.

If you have ever been filled with the Spirit, if you have ever received the gift of the Holy Spirit or baptism with the Holy Ghost (whatever term you want to use), then you have power in you right now.

You may be waiting to feel something. It has nothing to do with what you feel. **Now, I welcome feelings, but I don't base my faith on feelings.** My faith is based on God's Word, not on how I feel about it. God's Word is so, whether you feel like it or not. It only has to do with the fact that God has said it. That's what makes it so, because God cannot lie.

We want to find out ONLY what the Bible says about it. I'm not concerned about what you think. I'm not concerned about what your church teaches. I am only concerned with what God says. Now if what you think, what you say, and what your church teaches is the same thing that God says, fine, we can get it together. But, if not, I am sticking with God. I want to stick with God because His Word will never fail.

God Dwells In Man By His Spirit—

There is a very interesting statement in the Bible along these lines concerning the indwelling presence of the Spirit of God. God dwells in man by His Spirit. The Holy Spirit dwells in man to give him the supernatural power so that man can be a 24-hour-a-day overcomer, seven days a week. God wants you to be an overcomer.

In II Corinthians 6:16 it says, *"And what agreement hath the temple of God with idols? for ye are the temple of the living God; as God hath said; I will dwell in them, and walk in them; and I will be their God, and they shall be my people."* You see, your body is the temple in which God lives. God doesn't live in the church building. God doesn't live in the cathedral down the street. God lives in human bodies.

God is a Spirit, but God lives and manifests himself in and through human bodies. This verse says (I didn't write it), "And what agreement hath the temple of God with idols? for ye are the temple of the living God; as God hath said, I will dwell IN them and walk in them."

The Bible says, "Christ in you, the hope of glory" (Colossians 1:27). God is in you, but the way He is in you is by His Spirit — not by an emotion, not by a feeling but by His Spirit. God dwells and manifests himself through human beings. The Bible says that we are workers together with God. (II Corinthians 6:1.) God does not do anything in the earth realm apart from man. You need to understand that.

Lend Yourself As A Channel—

Are you waiting for God to do something? Are you waiting for God to come down and manifest himself in some kind of glory before you will believe it?

God works through human instrumentality. He works through YOU and He works through me. If we don't lend ourselves to Him as channels and vehicles, then He can't do anything in this earth realm.

Don't ask me why, because I don't know. I didn't make this thing, I found it when I got here. I found out that it works (God's Word), so I started getting in line with it and things started happening. Do you follow me?

Thank God, you don't have to know how it works to enjoy it, to benefit from it. If we had to know how everything works we wouldn't have anything to enjoy in this life, even in the natural world.

You don't understand everything in the natural world, but you don't have to understand everything to enjoy the benefits of it.

The Scripture says that God dwells in human temples. That is, **He dwells in you if you are a child of God.**

This junk about God being in everybody is erroneous. It's unscriptural. It is not in the Bible. There is an erroneous idea that God is the Father of all men and we are all brothers. That is not scripturally true. God is not the Father of all men. God is the creator of man, but He's not the Father of all men. There is no such thing as the Fatherhood of God and the Brotherhood of man. The only brothers I have are those in Christ. If you are not in Christ you are not my brother. You are only an acquaintance. That's Bible.

"But as many as received him, to them gave he power to become the sons of God, even to them that believe on his name: Which were born, not of blood, nor of the will of the flesh, nor of the will of man, but of God. And the Word was made flesh, and dwelt among us, (and we beheld his glory, the glory as of the only begotten of the Father,) full of grace and truth" (John 1:12-14).

This Scripture is talking about Jesus Christ who is the Word of God, who became flesh and dwelt among men. *"But as many as received him* (Jesus Christ), *to them gave he power* (authority) *to become the sons of God."*

Why would He have to give me authority to become something I already am? If I already am a child of God, then why does He need to give me authority to become something I already am?

For instance, I am a citizen of the United States of America. I was born in this country. I don't have to take out naturalization papers, I am a citizen. I was born into the family of the United States of America, so I don't have to have anybody give me any authority to become a citizen of the United States.

Now the man who comes from another nation, another country, has to become a naturalized citizen. In other words, he has to be adopted into the family since he is not native born.

The Scripture verse says, "But as many as received him, to them gave he power to become the sons of God." If they were already the sons of God, if God was their Father already, then they wouldn't need any authority to become something that they already were.

God is not the Father of everybody. He is only the Father of those who receive His Son Jesus Christ. Through Jesus Christ His Son they are given the authority to be adopted into His family. Then and only then can they call Him "Father."

There are a lot of people going around with this "Yahweh" business, the "tetragrammaton," the four letter word for God in the old Hebrew language (JHVH). They tell you that you have to call Him "Yahweh." That is because they don't really know God. He is just a stranger to them.

You don't call your father "John, or Joe, or Bill." You call him "Daddy." You call him "Papa." You call him "Father," because that's the relationship that you have with him.

The kid across the street doesn't call him "Father," he calls him "Mr. Jones."

The point I am trying to make is, when you come to know God as your heavenly Father, you don't have to call Him "Yahweh." You just call Him "Father!" Praise God.

Jesus said, "When you pray, say 'Our Father . . . .' " He also said, "Verily I say unto you, if you ask anything in my name, ask the Father, and He will give it to you."

God is our heavenly Father. If you have been adopted into the family of God, by receiving Jesus Christ as your personal Savior, He is your Father too. You are a son. That is the way you get in the family of God, the only way.

The Temple Of God—

"Know ye not that ye are the temple of God, and that the Spirit of God dwelleth in you" (I Corinthians 3:16). Paul is telling us that God lives in us. Our bodies are the temples of God.

Some people ask, "Now what's sin and what's not sin? What can I do and what can't I do?"

All you have to do is realize that God is living in you. If Jesus came to town, knocked on your door with His bags in His hands and said, "I am here to spend a week with you," what would you do?

You would start cleaning up the house and getting things together, hiding your bottles and your cards.

You would move the ash trays out of the way. You would run down to the store and get the best cut of meat. You would want to make a good impression on the Lord.

All of your neighbors, relatives and friends would come in, and as soon as they arrived you would meet them at the door, "Sh-sh-sh watch your mouth! The Lord's here, watch your mouth!"

Why?

Because you respect the presence of the Lord.

Friend, **God is in you.** How can you put pills in your body? How can you put strong drink in it that destroys you? How can you take nicotine? Those things rob your body. God is IN YOU, not outside of you.

If you ask, "What's sin, and what's not sin?" the answer is this: If you will do it in the church building (this is just a physical building), and He is not in the building, then do it in your body.

I see men walk up to the church and they throw their cigarettes away before they go into the church building. They wouldn't think of smoking a cigarette in the main sanctuary. Yet they will put it in their body, and that is where God is.

Our minds are so mixed up it's a wonder that we get anything done. You talk about smart. No, brother, man is dumb, he is not smart. We will reverence the church building, but pay little attention to our bodies. If I should suggest to the Executive Committee, "I think we ought to have a cocktail party in the main sanctuary," they would say, "Ahhh, Pastor, you don't mean that, do you?"

You don't mind having it at home in your body. You don't mind putting it in your body, and the Bible says that's where God lives — IN YOU!

We need to know the reality of the indwelling Spirit. When you realize that God is IN YOU, when you realize that He is in you by the power and presence of His Holy Spirit, it will go a long way toward helping you to walk the straight and narrow. You'll find that it's easy to be a Christian. It's easy to do the things that are right, if you want to do them.

Jesus said these very words. He is not a liar. *"Come unto me, all ye that labour and are heavy laden, and I will give you rest. Take my yoke upon you, and learn of me; for I am meek and lowly in heart: and ye shall find rest unto your souls. For my yoke is easy, and my burden is light"* (Matthew 11:28-30). If you say you have a heavy load then you are not walking in the light, because He said, "My yoke is easy and my burden if LIGHT." The reason that it is light is because Jesus carries it. If you still have a heavy load, get rid of it, give it to Jesus. Then, you'll walk around and have to hold on to things to keep from floating away, you'll be so light.

We already read that we are the temple of God, that the Spirit of God dwells in us. *"If any man defile the temple of God, him shall God destroy; for the temple of God is holy, which temple ye are"* (I Corinthians 3:17). If you are calling yourself a

Christian, you better get it together. If you say you are filled with the Spirit and you are doing all those unholy things, you better get it together. This verse told us, "If any man defiles God's house, God's going to catch up with him." You may hide it from mamma and papa, but you can't hide it from God. When the ax falls don't go crying, "Oh Lord have mercy on me!" Your body is the temple. It ought to be a holy place. It ought to be clean.

It feels good to be clean on the inside and the outside.

I have found that God's Word is really clear.

You may say, "Well, that's just your interpretation. I have my own interpretation."

Well, nobody told you to have your own interpretation. I am not giving you *my* interpretation. I am just reading Scripture. If you have a Bible, read it yourself, and you will see it too. This is the Word of God.

"What? know ye not that your body is the temple of the Holy Ghost which is in you, which ye have of God, and ye are not your own? For ye are bought with a price: therefore glorify God in your body, and in your Spirit, which are God's" (I Corinthians 6:19-20).

What do you think "body" means?

Your *body* is the temple of the Holy Ghost. It surely doesn't mean a sardine can! You wouldn't say that meant a space capsule! It doesn't mean a submarine. **Your body is the temple of the Holy Ghost**

which is in you. "Therefore glorify God in your body
. . . ." Now can you glorify God in your body when
your body is run down and functioning on only two
cylinders instead of eight? How can you glorify God
when your body is wracked with cancer and disease?
How could anybody ever think that sickness could be
God's perfect will? To believe this, one has to be
blinded by Satan.

Your body is the house that God lives in. You
don't even like to live in a house where the roof leaks.
What makes you think that God wants to live in one
with a roof that leaks? Yet, many of our houses are
leaking (as it were). Bad heart, bad liver, bad kidney,
bad eyes, bad ears, bad gums, bad feet; something's
always hurting. How in the world can God be glorified
that way?

God's house is supposed to have the best in it.
Your body ought to be right. You ought to be hearing
right and seeing right. My eyes get better by the day,
not weaker. They get better and my hair gets blacker.
That's right; I believe it! He said, "Every hair on your
head is numbered," and I expect to keep the same
number that I started out with, right down to the day
I die. I'll be in good health. Strong! I'll hear well, I'll
see well, I'll walk well, my arms and legs will function,
I won't have arthritis, because this is God's house and
He doesn't desire to live in any broken-down houses!

Even the kings of this world live in the best, don't
they? Their palaces are the best. Well, the King of
Kings lives in my body.

Notice again what he says, *"What? know ye not that your body is the temple of the Holy Ghost which is in you."* He is not out there. We have songs that we sing, "Come by here Lord, come by here," Glory to God, He is here! He doesn't have to come by here. God is here because we are here. He said He lives in us. He said, *". . . If two of you shall agree on earth as touching any thing that they should ask, it shall be done for them of my Father which is in heaven. For where two or three are gathered together in my name, there am I in the midst of them"* (Matthew 18:19-20).

He is here, because He said He's here. I don't have to **feel** anything or **see** anything. He said, "I am in the midst of you." He said, "I'll never leave you nor forsake you." (Hebrews 13:5.)

Because He's here, we can boldly say, "Whom shall we fear? God is with us, he is in us."

He said, "The Spirit of God is in us." HE IS IN US! Until you realize that and begin to rely on the Greater One, you will be ineffective as a channel of blessing.

Fred Price has no power, no ability, no understanding. I am nothing without Him, but He is in me, thank God. I have Him, because He said, *"Christ in you the hope of glory"* (Colossians 1:27). *"I can do all things through Christ which strengtheneth me"* (Philippians 4:13).

Rely On The Greater One—

I rely on the Greater One who dwells in me. He will forever be in me. He said, "I'll never leave you or forsake you." Praise God He is in me. "I'll give you the Holy Spirit and He'll be with you forever."

When you realize that He is in you, you will begin to rely on the Greater One. When you begin to say to Him, "Greater One, I need a little assistance right now. I can't do it myself. I need a little power," He will put it in overdrive, press down on the passing gear, and you will have the power you need to overcome every obstacle and every temptation. You can talk to God. He is a divine person.

He is in you NOW. You need to realize that. Stop singing, "Come by here Lord, come by here." He's here NOW! Stop talking about "pour out your Spirit on us." He has already poured HIM out. He has been here 1900 years. All you have to do is reach out by faith and receive.

The Truth Of God's Word Will Make You Free—

Thank God for the Word of God. Jesus said, "If ye continue in my word, then are ye my disciples indeed; And ye shall know the truth and the truth shall make you free." You see, it's the truth of God's Word that makes you free. REALLY FREE!

Many of you today are in bondage. You're all hung-up and strung-out; you don't know which way to go. You are trying to be cool, you may be sitting there with that cool grin on your face, but inside, you are a seething volcano.

You can be free.

There are many churches and denominations which teach that when you're born again, or what we call saved or converted, you at that time receive the gift of the Holy Spirit. They claim it's all the same as being saved. This is not Bible. It is NOT THE SAME.

Jesus is a gift. He is the gift of salvation, but the Holy Spirit is a gift also. He is a gift of power. You need both. You need salvation, and then you need the power to live that life of salvation in the power of God's Spirit and not in the power of your own intellect.

In the fourth chapter of John, we have the account of Jesus in Samaria. He came to a well and while He remained there at the well side, His disciples went into the city to buy bread. A harlot came down to the well in the middle of the day (high noon) to draw water.

Jesus asked the woman for a drink of water and she said, "Why do you ask me, a Samaritan, for a drink of water? for the Jews have no dealings with the Samaritans."

Jesus said to her, "If you knew who it was that was asking you for a drink of water, you would ask Him and He would give you living water."

She said, "Lord, where are you going to get the water. The well is deep and you don't have anything to draw the water from the well."

Then Jesus said this, in verse 14, *"But whosoever drinketh of the water that I shall give him shall never thirst; but the water that I shall give him shall be in him a well of water springing up into everlasting life."* Jesus is talking about salvation. He is talking about being born again. He is talking about becoming a new creature in Christ Jesus. That is an illustration of **salvation.** The spiritual life is typed as a well of water.

Now, look at John 7:37 and see if you can see a difference here. Jesus is speaking again, and He says this: *"In the last day, that great day of the feast, Jesus stood and cried, saying, If any man thirst, let him come unto me, and drink. He that believeth on me, as the scripture hath said, out of his belly* (innermost being) *shall flow rivers of living water. (But this spake he of the Spirit, which they that believe on him should receive: for the Holy Ghost was not yet given; because that Jesus was not yet glorified.)"*

I thank God that Jesus interprets this Scripture. We can't mess it up. He told us what it meant. He said, *"But this spake he of the Spirit, which they that believe on him should receive."* He didn't say they **would** receive, He said they **should** receive, because it isn't automatic.

Rivers Of Living Water—

Can you see a difference in a "WELL" and "RIVERS?" Is there a difference between a well and rivers?

He told the woman at the well, "The water that I give you (water is symbolic of spiritual life) shall be in you a well of water springing up into everlasting life."

Then Jesus says that when we receive the gift of the Holy Spirit, out of our innermost beings shall flow "rivers of living water."

You can live off a well, in terms of it sustaining you with water. You can drink the water from that well, and you sustain life, but you know what you can't do with a well? You can't do any work with a well, because still water cannot produce any power. However, when you have rivers flowing, you can turn wheels and you can generate power. **Moving water produces power**, but a well doesn't have any power. It can give you life but it can't do any work.

God wants you filled with the Spirit so you can have more than just life. Jesus said, "I came that they might have life, and have it more abundantly." (John 10:10)

You can't have life abundant unless you have power. In the 14th chapter of John, Jesus is talking to His disciples at Jerusalem about His soon departure. Jesus had been their Comforter. He had been their friend. He had been their confidant. They could go to Jesus for anything they needed. He fed them, encouraged them, salved their fear; He did everything for them. He was with them all the time. But now, He is getting ready to physically and visibly leave them. He says, *"And I will pray the Father, and he shall give you another Comforter, that he may abide with you forever"* (verse 16).

The names "Comforter, Holy Ghost, Holy Spirit, Spirit of Truth, and Spirit of God," are all (for want of a better term) **aliases** for one and the same person: the **third person of the Trinity**. When you see the word *Comforter* it means the Holy Spirit, and it shows forth an aspect of His personality and work. It literally means "paraclete" in the Greek, or "paracleton," which means helper or assistant. Jesus was telling them that He was not going to leave them comfortless. He was going to give them somebody to help them, to assist in the things of God. That is the Holy Spirit.

YOU MUST RECEIVE HIM. *"Even the Spirit of truth; whom the world cannot receive, because it seeth him not, neither knoweth him: but ye know him: for he dwelleth with you, and shall be IN YOU"* (verse 17). The Day of Pentecost was the day He would be in them.

Right when Jesus was talking, the Holy Ghost was with them, because Jesus was with them. He was filled with the Spirit, so the Holy Ghost was with them. But there was coming a day when He would not only be **with** them, but He would be IN them and that was on the Day of Pentecost.

The statement that Jesus made is prophetic. Notice, it says that the world cannot receive Him. The world represents sinners; it represents those who are not in the family of God. So what the Bible is saying is that a sinner cannot receive the Holy Spirit.

That shoots down the doctrine that says when you receive Jesus Christ as your personal Savior you are automatically filled with the Holy Ghost at that same moment. You are not. This verse says that the world can't receive Him.

Let me ask you a question. What are you prior to your receiving Jesus Christ as your personal Savior?

You are a sinner. That means that when you receive Jesus Christ you are as a sinner receiving Christ.

Well, if you receive the gift of the Holy Spirit at the same point in time, then that also would mean that you are as a sinner receiving the Holy Spirit. He just said, the world CAN'T receive Him, didn't He?

That means that a sinner cannot receive the gift of the Holy Spirit.

You have to become a Christian **before** you are even *eligible* to receive the gift of the Holy Spirit. Now you can receive Christ one minute and you can receive the gift of the Holy Spirit the next minute, but you can't receive both of them at the same time. For instance, you can't receive Jesus and the Holy Ghost at one minute after twelve. You have to receive one at one after twelve and then you may receive the other at one minute and one second after twelve, but you can't receive both of them at the same time. One has to precede the other.

You have to have life before you start breathing. You have to be redeemed before you can receive the gift of the Holy Spirit.

The Holy Spirit Is The Gift—

We hear people saying, "Oh, I received the baptism." Actually that's an unscriptural term to use. There is no baptism *of* the Holy Spirit offered to you.

There is the GIFT OF THE HOLY SPIRIT. **He** is offered to you, but not *the baptism*. Let's see what the Bible says about it. John the Baptist was preaching and baptizing people in water. People wanted to know, "Who are you anyway? Who gave you the authority to do what you are doing?"

John the Baptist told them, *"I indeed baptize you with water unto repentance: but he that cometh after me,* (he was referring to Jesus) *is mightier than I, whose shoes I am not worthy to bear: he shall baptize you* **with** *the Holy Ghost, and with fire"* (Matthew 3:11).

Notice, JESUS WILL BAPTIZE **WITH** THE HOLY GHOST.

Let's look at Mark's version of the same account of John the Baptist. *"I indeed have baptized you with water: but he shall baptize you* **with** *the Holy Ghost"* (Mark 1:8). He is saying that Jesus shall baptize **with**, WITH the Holy Ghost.

We read of the same account in Luke 3:16. *"John answered, saying unto them all, I indeed baptize you*

*with water; but one mightier than I cometh, the
latchet of whose shoes I am not worthy to unloose: he
shall baptize you* **with** *the Holy Ghost and with fire."*

Did you notice, in each one of these cases it says
that Jesus will baptize *with* the Holy Ghost?

We do see that the term, "baptism with the Holy
Ghost," is a biblical term, but what we want to do is
put it in its proper context. We want to use the term
properly.

When people say, "I received the baptism," that is
really unscriptural. They didn't receive *the baptism.*
They received the Holy Ghost, the Holy Spirit. And
the process by which they received the Holy Spirit is
JESUS **baptizing** WITH THE HOLY GHOST. But
that's not WHAT YOU RECEIVED. WHAT you
received WAS THE HOLY SPIRIT.

When you are baptized by the church, in water,
they put you into the water. It is not the water you
receive, is it? The water is what you are put into.
Actually you are receiving *baptism;* it is one of the
ordinances of the church. The water is the element by
which you are baptized.

Now look at this. This is John the Baptist talking
again. He says, *"And I knew him not: but he that sent
me to baptize with water, the same said unto me,
Upon whom thou shalt see the Spirit descending, and
remaining on him, the same is he which baptizeth* **with**
the Holy Ghost" (John 1:33).

In Acts 1:4-5, Jesus is speaking just before He went back to heaven after His resurrection. *"And, being assembled together with them, commanded them that they should not depart from Jerusalem, but wait for the promise of the Father, which saith he, ye have heard of me. For John truly baptized with water; but ye shall be baptized* **with** *the Holy Ghost not many days hence."*

Please keep in mind that in the above verses, Jesus was talking to the disciples, and Peter was one of those disciples. Now, let's read what Peter said in the 11th chapter of Acts, verses 15 and 16: "And as I began to speak, the Holy Ghost fell on them, as on us at the beginning. Then remembered I the word of the Lord, how that he said, John indeed baptized with water; but ye shall be baptized with the Holy Ghost" (Acts 11:15-16).

I want to show you by the Scripture that it is not the *baptism* with the Holy Ghost that is offered to you. Remember, God is merely saying what Jesus will do. Jesus will baptize with the Holy Ghost. That is God's part of the proposition. Man's part is to receive the gift!

In the 2nd chapter of Acts, after the Holy Spirit had come and the 120 in the upper room were filled with the Holy Ghost, speaking with other tongues, they went downstairs under the power of the Holy Spirit. They were filled with the Holy Ghost, and they came staggering down the stairs under the power. Some people saw them coming down and accused them of being drunk. They said, "These men are full of new wine, they've been nipping at the bottle too long."

Finally Peter stood up and said, *"No, these are not drunken, as ye suppose, seeing it is but the third hour of the day. But this is that which was spoken by the prophet Joel."* Peter went on and preached a sermon. Now nobody was converted while they were speaking in tongues. (Speaking in tongues has its rightful place, but it's not used to convert men.) Only the Word of God can get men converted: You have to be born of the *Spirit* and the *Word.*

"Now when they heard this, they were pricked in their heart, and said unto Peter and to the rest of the apostles, Men and brethren, what shall we do? Then Peter said unto them, Repent, and be baptized every one of you in the name of Jesus Christ for the remission of sins, and ye shall receive the gift of the Holy Ghost" (Acts 2:37-38).

Remember, God has done His part. It's up to YOU to do something about what God has done. He has already spoken. He has already acted. He has already given. He has already offered. He has already promised. BUT YOU HAVE TO BELIEVE IT, AND BY FAITH RECEIVE IT; then it becomes active in your own life.

When they said, "What shall we do?" Peter said to them, "repent." That means to turn away from your old life and turn to the Lord Jesus Christ. "Repent, and be baptized every one of you." That's water baptism which is an outward sign of an inward grace.

It's symbolic of our dying to the old man. When something dies you bury it, so you immerse it under the water, which is a symbol of being buried with Christ. When you come up out of the waters of baptism, that represents resurrection into a new life.

Peter said, *"Repent, and be baptized every one of you in the name of Jesus Christ for the remission of sins, and ye shall receive the gift of the Holy Ghost."*

Peter calls it "the gift." If anything is a gift, then that pre-supposes two things that are very important. First of all, in order for me to benefit from the gift, **the gift has to be offered to me.** Secondly, it never becomes mine until **I receive it.**

Something can be offered to me and I can reject it. I don't have to receive it, but it will never become mine until I receive it. Right?

Take The Whole Gift—

Let's look at something else. Peter had seen a vision, and God told him to go down and minister the Word at the home of Cornelius, a Gentile.

"While Peter yet spake. these words, the Holy Ghost fell on all them which heard the word. And they of the circumcision which believed were astonished, as many as came with Peter, because that on the Gentiles also was poured out the gift of the Holy Ghost. For they heard them speak with tongues, and magnify God" (Acts 10:44-46).

That's what convinced the early church that the people were Spirit-filled: *"For they heard them speak with tongues."*

Perhaps you have a **hang-up** concerning speaking with other tongues (many do). You don't mind the Holy Ghost, but you don't want anything to do with "tongues."

I'll tell you, when somebody gives you a present, you get the wrapping paper, the ribbon, and the card, plus what's in the box, or you don't get anything. When somebody gives you a gift you don't say, "I don't want the wrapping paper. Take the wrapping paper off. I don't want the card or the ribbon."

No. You say, "Thank you!" and take everything, don't you?

Well, friend, the "tongues" goes with the package. They have their place. Praise God!

"For they heard them speak with tongues, and magnify God." Tongues are used primarily to magnify God in your own private devotional life. There is also an aspect of tongues which is public, a public manifestation of tongues with interpretation.

In verse 47 Peter says, *"Can any man forbid water, that these should not be baptized, which have received the Holy Ghost as well as we?"* They had received the Holy Ghost. Notice, they had received. Received what? They had RECEIVED THE HOLY GHOST.

The Holy Ghost has been poured out already, but many are not receiving. They are too **cool** to receive. They would rather tough it out in their own strength. But as for me, give me God's power. There's no other way to go but the power of God.

The Responsibility Is Yours—

The responsibility for being filled with the Holy Spirit is on YOU. YOU have to receive. Some people will say, "Well, if God wants me filled with the Holy Ghost, He'll just have to fill me. If He wants me to speak in tongues He will just have to open my mouth!"

You will be sitting there until hell freezes over (and it's not about to do that) if that is the way you feel.

Acts 8:14-17 says, *"Now when the apostles which were at Jerusalem heard that Samaria had received the word of God, they sent unto them Peter and John: Who, when they were come down, prayed for them, that they might receive the Holy Ghost: (For as yet he was fallen upon none of them: only they were baptized in the name of the Lord Jesus.) Then laid they their hands on them, and they received the Holy Ghost."* Notice, "That THEY MIGHT RECEIVE," not that God might give, but that they might receive. That's their responsibility; it's your responsibility to receive.

Let's look at this passage, "For as yet he was fallen upon none of them: only they were baptized in the name of the Lord Jesus." You can be genuinely **born again, genuinely saved, genuinely baptized in**

water, and you are as much a Christian as you are
ever going to be. If you were to live a thousand years,
you wouldn't be any more born again than you are
right now. If you are never filled with the Holy Ghost
and speak with tongues, you are still a Christian, and
if you die before Jesus returns, you will go right on to
glory to be with Him.

You may ask, "Well, what's the point in being
filled with the Holy Ghost?"

For power. For SUPERNATURAL POWER, so
that the works of God can be done by the Spirit of God
in divine power.

Too many of the things that we do are done in our
own strength. It is one thing to be "**born of the
Spirit**," and it's another to be "**filled with the Spirit**." I
believe that these verses that we just read show us
very clearly there is a difference.

Notice verse 16 again, "For as yet he (the **Holy
Spirit**) was fallen upon none of them: only they were
baptized in the name of the Lord Jesus." Remember,
Phillip was one of those chosen to be a deacon. I'm
sure that he would have known what constituted being
born again. He would not have baptized these
Samaritans unless they had given proof of their
acceptance of Christ as Lord and Savior. Not only
that, but if being "**filled with the Holy Spirit**" was the
same thing as "**being born again**," there would be no
need to point out the fact that "He (the Holy Ghost)
had fallen upon none of them." This shows us that
receiving Christ as Savior and receiving the gift of the

Holy Ghost are two different transactions. Verse 17 tells us, "Then laid they their hands on them, and they received the Holy Ghost."

Notice it said, "they received." It did not say that "God gave."

The responsibility for being filled with the Spirit is not on God, but on us. He has already **given.** It is up to us to **receive.** Once we receive the gift of the Holy Ghost, it is up to us to recognize the fact that He, the Greater One, is now in us. Once you recognize that as a living reality — you have supernatural ability resident in you — your faith will be strong.

God has given us His Spirit. "Greater is he that is in you, than he that is in the world." I thank God that the Greater One lives in me today. I thank God I don't have to preach by the power of Fred Price, but I preach by the power of the Holy Spirit. I don't have to lay hands on anybody in my power. I put hands on them in the NAME OF JESUS! And Jesus said, "These signs shall follow them that believe, in my name they shall lay hands on the sick and they shall recover."

I am against sickness. I am against disease. I am against the devil. I am against demons. I am against poverty.

I am for riches. I am for power and I am for God, because **God is power, God is life** and **God is Spirit.** He said, "My word shall go forth and shall not return to me void." (Isaiah 55:11.) He said, "Not by might, nor by

power, but by my spirit, saith the Lord of hosts"
(Zechariah 4:6).

You now have principle number five: **You must
Know the Reality of the Indwelling Spirit.**

6

Know the Reality of the Authority of the Name of Jesus

Now we come to the final chapter which discusses a very important principle with you. Principle number six: You must **Know the Reality of the Authority of the Name of Jesus.**

Jesus Gave Us That Authority—

The body of Christ needs to understand and come to grips with the fact that there is authority in the name of Jesus. It is by that name, and through that name that you have your victory, THE NAME OF JESUS!

The name of Jesus is a name that I highly treasure.

There is healing in the name of Jesus.

You must KNOW that there is authority in that NAME OF JESUS. You must KNOW it as a reality. You must know it, not as an idea, not as a philosophy, not as a hope, not as a dream, but YOU MUST KNOW THAT NAME AS AN ACTUAL, LIVING, VITAL REALITY. **You must Know the Reality of the Authority of the Name of Jesus Christ.**

We are going to examine (just as we have done in the five previous chapters concerning each principle) what the Bible says about the authority of the Name of Jesus. We do not want to be too concerned about what the denominations teach, or what the professors say, or what tradition says. We want to KNOW WHAT GOD'S WORD SAYS about it. What does the Bible have to say?

I know that many of you who read this book believe that the Bible is a strange book. Perhaps you have been in the church for 20, 30 or 40 years, and yet the Bible is like reading Greek. You don't have the slightest notion or idea about what is in the Bible. You have been going along by how you feel. If it sounded good and tickled your ears, it was a good sermon. If it made you feel **goose-bumpy** all over and made you feel like you wanted to run and shout, then it was a wonderful message. It didn't matter too much what the content of the message was, it didn't matter too much if the message was grounded in the authority of God's Word, as long as it sounded all right, you accepted it.

That day is gone, friend; that is a thing of the past. Jesus said, "The truth will make you free."

Thank God, today I am free. I want you to find the same truths that I have found, so that you too can be free and then you can go out into this sin-cursed world and set men free.

You see, Jesus could only be in one geographical location at a time. He could only minister to one group of people at a time, so He chose 70 disciples to help Him in His ministry. He sent them out in different directions. He multiplied himself 70 times over. Instead of ministering to one person, actually 71 people could be ministered to at the same time in different parts of the country. They had gone out and had been very successful in their ministry. They came back to report to Jesus what had happened.

"And the seventy returned again with joy, saying, Lord, even the devils are subject unto us through thy name. And he said unto them, I beheld Satan as lightning fall from heaven. Behold, I give unto you power to tread on serpents and scorpions, and over all the power of the enemy: and nothing shall by any means hurt you" (Luke 10:17-19).

Notice the word *power* appears twice in verse 19. These words are not translated to their fullest extent. They do not give you the fullest impact of the meaning of what Jesus was saying when it was recorded in the what Jesus was saying when it was recorded in the original Greek. The first word *power* in verse 19 is the Greek word *exousia*, and the word means *authority*. The second word *power* in that same Scripture verse is the word *dunamous* in the Greek and it means *ability*. So if you read that in a literal translation, this is what it would say, "Behold, I give unto you authority to tread on serpents and scorpions, and over all the ability of the enemy; and nothing shall by any means hurt you." Now, isn't that stronger?

It says, "I have given you authority over all of the ability of the enemy." That means that the authority that you as a Christian have at your disposal is greater than the ability of the enemy. Then He says, "Nothing shall by any means hurt you."

Can't you see that 90% of the Christians are not walking in the light of this Word, because they are being hurt and harmed all the time by Satan? Yet Jesus said, "Nothing shall hurt you, because I've given you this authority."

Authority To Ask Or Demand In The Name Of Jesus—

Authority is of no value unless you act on that authority. You can have the keys to the kingdom, but if you don't open the door, it won't do you any good. You have to open the door.

The Church has this authority but it hasn't known it. It has been satisfied to feed on the **fruits of emotionalism and traditionalism.** The Church has been satisfied to feed on the **dry husks of philosophy** and to eat at the **slop-tray of theology.** Consequently, the Church has not known its rights, and the devil has lorded it over us.

Thank God, Satan's through lording it over me! I know what God said. He said, "I have given you authority to tread on serpents and scorpions." Serpents and scorpions are symbolic terms for part of the encampment of the enemy. He says, "on serpents and scorpions, and over all of the ability of the enemy." Not **some** of it, but over **all** of it. I have that, because I have the NAME OF JESUS.

We are going to study two Scripture passages which I believe will show you something in the light of the Word. They will be of great value to you.

In the first passage, Jesus was making a statement to His disciples. You need to realize that when Jesus talked to those that He had chosen to send out, He was not only talking directly to them, but also, He was talking to those who would believe, as a result of their ministry. That means that He was talking to us too! He was talking to them; they, in turn, would go and tell others, who would, in turn, go and tell others. Eventually it came to me; and I, in turn, am telling you!

Now the job that God wants you to do is go tell somebody else. Pass it on! That's the name of the game.

Jesus said, *"Verily, verily, I say unto you, He that believeth on me, the works that I do shall he do also; and greater works than these shall he do; because I go unto my Father. And whatsoever ye shall ask in my name, that will I do, that the Father may be glorified in the Son. If ye shall ask any thing in my name, I will do it"* (John 14:12-14).

Any time you see double "verily's" in the Gospels, you know that Jesus is getting ready to make a momentous statement. He is getting ready to say something that is of vital importance to you; so He is using "verily, verily" to capture your attention. He is saying, **"Truly, truly,** I say unto you, He that believes on Me, the works that I do shall he do in addition to what I have done; and greater works than these shall he do because I go to My Father."

Jesus said that we would be able to do the works that He did. You can see why we will be able to do them when you look back at Luke 10. He just said, "I give unto you **authority** over all the **ability** of the enemy." That is the reason we can do the works that Jesus did. We have the authority to use His name.

When we use His name, we have what is called in the legal profession, "the power of attorney." That means that when we use His name, it is just as though He did it himself. We do it **in lieu**, or we **act on behalf of Him**. We use His name and His name has authority in it. It is as if He himself were to use that name. "The works that I do shall you do also."

Somebody said, "Miracles and healings went out with the early church."

That verse we just read doesn't look like it, does it? He said, "The works that I do shall you do also."

What were the works that Jesus did?

He raised the dead. He opened the eyes of the blind. He unstopped deaf ears. He cast out demons. He stopped the waters. He cursed the fig tree. He made bread. He did all of those things. And He said, "The works I do shall you do also (or in addition to)."

Somebody said, "Oh, I don't believe that is for us today!"

That is exactly why it hasn't worked. You won't believe it. You are sitting there saying, "I don't believe it."

Jesus said it would! He said, "The works that I do shall you do also and greater works than these shall you do." He doesn't mean greater in *quality*. He means greater in *quantity* because there are more of us than there were of Jesus. He was only one man. There are millions of Christians.

If all the millions of Christians would minister to one blind person, a million blind people could be healed instantly. Jesus could only be in one place at one time. We can be all over the world. He didn't mean greater in quality, He meant greater in quantity. Jesus raised the dead. After you raise the dead, you can't do anything greater than that. There't nothing left to do after you raise the dead. That is the ultimate.

Look again at verses 13 and 14. *"And whatsoever ye shall ask in my name, that will I do, that the Father may be glorified in the Son. If ye shall ask any thing in my name, I will do it."*

When we do something in Jesus' name, it is as though He himself did it. He is not talking about prayer. He said, "If you ask anything in my name . . . ." He didn't say, "Ask the Father to give you something in My name." He said, "Ask any thing in My name and I will do it."

I will show you how this works. It is not prayer. Remember, He said, "If you shall ask any thing." Some Greek scholars say the word *ask* carries with it the connotation of demand. You are demanding something. **You are demanding your rights.** Now you are not demanding it of God; you are demanding it of the devil. It is the devil who has people in bondage. It's the devil who has men sick. It's the devil who has men in poverty. Therefore, what Jesus is telling us to do is this: We ask or demand in the name of Jesus that the devil take his hands off our property, off our family, off our finances, and off our bodies. Jesus is saying that the devil has to do it, because Jesus' name is the greatest name in the heavens, in the earth, and under the earth. The demons have to bow to His name. They have to do His bidding, because Jesus' name is a name above all names.

Praise God! Jesus has given us the authority to use His name!

Let's see how some men in the early church caught the meaning of this and did exactly what Jesus said.

"Now Peter and John went up together into the temple at the hour of prayer, being the ninth hour.

"And a certain man lame from his mother's womb was carried, whom they laid daily at the gate of the temple which is called Beautiful, to ask alms of them that entered into the temple;

"Who seeing Peter and John about to go into the temple asked an alms.

"And Peter, fastening his eyes upon him with John, said, Look on us.

"And he gave heed unto them, expecting to receive something of them.

"Then Peter said, Silver and gold have I none; but such as I have give I thee: In the name of Jesus Christ of Nazareth rise up and walk.

"And he took him by the right hand, and lifted him up: and immediately his feet and ankle bones received strength.

"And he leaping up stood, and walked, and entered with them into the temple, walking, and leaping and praising God" (Acts 3:1-8).

What a pitiful condition! He was born lame, never walked a day in his life, and he was more than forty years old. Think of it, forty years and the best he could do was sit at the side of the road with a tin cup in his hand and beg. That is tragic. That's pathetic.

He saw Peter and John about to go into the temple. He begged for something, "asked an alm." Then in verse 4, Peter with John fastened his eyes upon the man. The reason Peter told the man to look on them was to arrest the man's attention. Verse 5 tells us that the man **gave heed**. He **expected to receive** something from them.

The reason many Christians never get their prayers answered, the reason they suffer through life with sickness and bodily injuries, bodily ailments and diseases, is because they don't EXPECT to receive anything from God. They are only hoping that they are going to get something.

The passage we just read didn't say that this man looked upon them "hoping." It said he looked upon them EXPECTING TO GET SOMETHING. He expected. He had asked, "give me alms." When the man asked, they said, "look on us," and he looked expecting. The Bible says, "And he gave heed unto them." In other words he did what they said. He looked upon them; he expected to receive something from them.

Then Peter said, "Silver and gold have I none; but such as I have give I thee: In the name of Jesus Christ of Nazareth rise up and walk." When Peter took him by the right hand and lifted him up, he was healed immediately! He leaped up, stood, walked, and went into the temple with Peter and John, walking, and leaping, and praising God!

That is what Jesus means in the 14th chapter of John when He says, **"If you ask anything in my name, I will do it."** That's what Peter did. Peter was demanding of the devil, in Jesus' name, to take his hands off the lame man's body. And the man was made whole.

Peter didn't pray. He didn't get down on his knees and say, "Heavenly Father, we come to thee now Lord, thou art the hope of all generations, before the mountains were ever brought forth or before thou had formed the earth and the world, even from everlasting to everlasting, thou art God. Help us Lord!" No. Peter said, "In the name of Jesus Christ of Nazareth, rise and walk."

Do you see? They weren't praying. They were **using the authority of the NAME OF JESUS!**

We have that same authority, but it won't work for us because we won't believe it. We are afraid; we don't want anybody to call us a **religious fanatic.** If you go to church twice a week, you're a **religious nut.** They will say that it's all right for you to go once. That's acceptable. That's **par** for the course, but if you go two or three times, you have gone off the deep end!

Jesus said, "The works that I do shall you do also." He said, "If you ask any thing in my name, I will do it." It was just as though Jesus stood there in the place of Peter and took that man by the hand. Peter didn't say, "In my name." He didn't say, "In the name of the church." He didn't say, "In the name of Judaism," but he said, "In the name of Jesus Christ of Nazareth, rise and walk." Peter was demanding that the devil take his hands off that man's body — it was the devil who had the man in bondage. God honored HIS WORD.

What we just saw was how the name of Jesus is used in ministry. Peter used the name of Jesus in ministry, and the man rose and walked, because Peter had authority to use the NAME OF JESUS.

Jesus said, "I give you authority." BUT you have to use that authority. If you don't use it, it won't work for you. If you have missed it, it is because you have been waiting for God to do something and *then* you will believe He did it. God wants you to do exactly what Jesus said that you could do: **Use the authority of the name of Jesus and whip the devil.**

Authority To Use The Name Of Jesus In Prayer—

Now, we want to see how the name of Jesus is used in prayer.

Jesus said: *"Ye have not chosen me, but I have chosen you, and ordained you, that ye should go and bring forth fruit, and that your fruit should remain: that whatsoever ye shall ask of the Father in my name, he may give it you"* (John 15:16).

You can see that that is different from the scripture that we read in John 14:14 where Jesus said, "If ye shall ask any thing in my name, I will do it." In one verse, He says, "whatsoever ye shall ask of the Father in my name, **he may give it you.**" In John 14:14, He said "**I will do it.**" The Scripture verse in John 14:14 is not talking about prayer. He is talking about using the name of Jesus to minister with. But in John 15 He is telling you how to pray. He is telling you to ask the Father in His (Jesus') name and He (The Father) will give it you. There is a difference.

First we saw how we can use the name of Jesus to demand Satan to take his hands off somebody or some thing; now we are going to see how we can use the name of Jesus in prayer.

When you pray, you are wasting your time if you ask Jesus for anything. That isn't how you pray. You do not pray to Jesus. You can worship Him. You can adore Him. You can tell Him how much you love Him. You can praise His name, and all of that, but when it comes to asking for things, t-h-i-n-g-s! you have to ask the FATHER, in the name of Jesus.

The reason that many of us are not receiving the things that we desire is we won't be obedient. The Lord wants you to be obedient. Being obedient means to do what He says, not what you want to do. Do what He says, then it will work for you.

"And in that day ye shall ask me nothing. Verily, verily, I say unto you, Whatsoever ye shall ask the Father in my name, he will give it you. Hitherto have ye asked nothing in my name: ask, and ye shall receive, that your joy may be full" (John 16:23-24). Jesus is saying, "Don't ask Me anything."

Understand, at that time Jesus was with the disciples, and anything that they needed, they asked Him. One day, the tax collector came to Peter and asked, "Does your master pay taxes?"

Peter went in to Jesus; but before he could say anything, Jesus stopped him, "Now listen, who do men take taxes of, of their own children or of strangers?"

Peter said, "Of the strangers."

Then Jesus said, "Do the children go free? Well lest we offend them, go down to the ocean and drop a hook in the water and the first fish that comes up, you will find a piece of money in its mouth. Take that money and pay taxes for you and me." (Matthew 17:24-27.)

When they wanted bread, they said, "Master, we don't have anything to eat."

Jesus said, "What do you have?"

They answered, "Well, there is a little boy here and he has a few barley loaves and some fish, but what is that among so many?" At that time there were 4,000 men, not counting the women and children.

Jesus had them all sit down on the grass. He took the bread, looked up to heaven, broke the bread and it began growing! It began to multiply!

You say, "Oh, I don't believe that. I don't see how He could do that."

He didn't ask you to see how He did it. He just asked you to believe it.

I have seen miracles many times. I've seen legs grow out. It's the same power that made the bread grow that makes the leg, bone, sinew, flesh, ligaments, and muscles grow. If Jesus can make a leg grow, He can make a loaf of bread grow. He multiplied the bread, and it grew, and they fed them until they were full. Then they took up 12 baskets full of leftovers on one occasion.

While Jesus was there with the disciples, He supplied their every need. They didn't have to get on welfare; they didn't have to get on the county. All they had to do was ask Jesus because He was right there, physically ready to meet their needs.

But now Jesus was getting ready to (physically, visibly) leave them. Jesus had ministered under the Old Covenant, but the Old Covenant was getting ready to come to a close. The new day was ready to be ushered in. He said, *"And in that day,* (in that new day, in that New Covenant Day) *ye shall ask me nothing . . . Whatsoever ye shall ask the Father in my name, He will give it you. Hitherto have ye asked nothing in my name; ask, and ye shall receive, that your joy may be full"* (John 16:23-24).

That is the formula for prayer. If you say that you don't know how to pray, that's it right there. You have just been told by Jesus. That's all there is to it. All the "thee's" and "thou's" are not necessary. Starting every prayer with, "Our Father which art in heaven, Hallowed be thy name," is not necessary. Jesus said, **"Ask the Father for what you want, in my name, and the Father will give it to you."**

You don't have to be on your knees to do it. You don't have to be at the altar to do it. You don't have to be dressed a certain way when you pray.

Jesus told you to ask the Father in His (Jesus') name, and you will receive that your joy may be full.

God wants your joy full.

You can't have full joy when your body is wracked with pain. You can't have full joy when the doctor says, "There's nothing else we can do for you. We'll just have to send you home and let you die." Your joy can't be full when you can't feed your family, can't pay your bills, or meet your obligations. There is no joy there. But He said, *that your joy might be full.*

There Is A Qualifier—

You have to understand that all of these Scriptures that we have been reading are addressed to those who not only are Christians but also are **walking in the light of the Word.**

You can't do your own thing, then run in there real quick, when you get into trouble and the hatchet's about to fall on your neck and say, "Well, Lord, give me an extra hundred dollars, these people are getting ready to foreclose on me." That won't work.

These promises are made to those Christians who are walking in the light. Now I didn't say, "perfect." I didn't say, "They are without sin." I said, **"Those who are walking in the light of His Word."** It is only then that you can pray this way and EXPECT TO GET AN ANSWER.

If you are going to do your own thing, and think you are going to pray this prayer and get an answer, you might as well twiddle your thumbs because you won't get anything. There is a qualifier. Jesus tells us, **"If ye abide in me, and my words abide in you, ye shall ask what ye will, and it shall be done unto you"** (John 15:7).

The reason that He can give you that carte blanche is because (notice the prerequisite), there is a qualifier, **IF**. "If ye abide." The word *abide* in the Greek means to "live in; take up residence; settle down in." It doesn't mean hitting the church door once every six months. It doesn't mean dropping a nickel in the offering plate and think you are going to get by. Jesus said, "If ye abide in me, and my words abide in you (settle down, live in, take up residence in, live there, stay there, sleep there, eat there), ye shall ask what ye will, and it shall be done unto you." It will be done.

DON'T FORGET THE FINE PRINT! You do the Bible just like you do an automobile contract. You didn't read the fine print where the man said, "If you don't keep up the payments, we will reposses the car." Then when you are three months in arrears, you get mad because the man is coming to get it.

If you had read the fine print, it would have told you that if you didn't pay the payments, they would come and repossess it. All you have to do is pay the payments and you can keep it.

God's Word works the same way. There is quite a bit of fine print in the Bible. If you weren't so busy reading the sports page, the T.V. Guide, and many others that I won't even mention, you would know what God's will is because you would be abiding in His Word. When you do this, then you can ask what you will and He said you will have it.

I remind you, we are talking about the Reality of the Authority of the Name of Jesus.

There are many people today who despise that name. There are many people who don't think too highly of the name of Jesus. But one day, whether they want to or not, their knee is going to bow at that name. Their tongue is going to confess that Jesus Christ is Lord, to the glory of God.

In the 28th chapter of Matthew, Jesus was getting ready to go back to heaven. *"Then the eleven disciples went away into Galilee, into a mountain where Jesus appointed them. And when they saw him, they worshipped him: but some doubted.*

"And Jesus came and spake unto them, saying, **All power** *is given unto me in heaven and in earth. Go ye therefore, and teach all nations, baptizing them in the name of the Father, and of the Son, and of the Holy Ghost: Teaching them to observe all things whatsoever I have commanded you: and, lo, I am with you alway, even unto the end of the world"* (verses 16-20).

The word *power* in the above scripture is the word *exousia* in the Greek, and it means all **authority**. All of it, not some of it, not a little bit of it, but every bit of it. He is saying, "I have all authority in My hands."

When He says, "go ye therefore," the word *therefore* is saying that whatever He said in the previous verse is the premise. **Therefore,** based on that premise, He says, "Go ye therefore, and teach all nations, baptizing them in the name of the Father, and of the Son, and of the Holy Ghost: Teaching them to observe all things whatsoever I have commanded you: and, lo, I am with you alway, even unto the end of the world." He said, "ALL AUTHORITY in the heavens and in the earth is in my hands. I have it right there."

The Bible says that Jesus is presently, geographically speaking, seated at the right hand of the Majesty on High. Jesus is seated at His Father's right hand in the heavenly places.

There is no scriptural evidence anywhere in the Bible, from Genesis to Revelation, that in the last 1900 years since Jesus went back to heaven, that He has ever had any need or any use for His name on this earth, because He is seated in heaven.

He left His body on the earth. He left the Church here on the earth and all of the authority, in the earth realm, Jesus delegated it to His body (the Church). That goes right along with the scripture that we read in Luke 10:19 where Jesus said, "I give unto you power (authority) to tread on serpents and scorpions, and over all the power (ability) of the enemy: and nothing shall by any means hurt you."

The Church (the body of Christ) has been left in the earth and we have the power of attorney to use the name of Jesus. We (the Church, the body of Christ) have the authority to use that name. That name of Jesus works for me; I use it, and He said that it will work for you too.

Grasp The Truth—

Remember, He said, "ALL authority is given unto Me." He said, "I'm getting ready to go back to heaven." The cloud took Him up and He said, "I'm leaving my body on earth. I give all the authority in the earth realm to my body, the Church."

Praise God! We have all of the authority in the earth. If you could only grasp that truth!

Jesus said, "Go teach." That's what I'm doing. I have a teaching ministry. You can't do too much shouting off my kind of preaching. It isn't geared to make you feel good; it is geared to inform you so that you can come out from under the hammer of the enemy. You might feel good for a few minutes, but as soon as you walk out the church door, the devil is going to be right there; then, "**whop**," down you go. That feeling is not going to help you. But if you can get what I am telling you, when those things come against you, you can point your finger in the face of the devil and say, "Listen, in the name of Jesus get out of my life. Get out of my house. Take your hands off my family, and off my finances, and off my job. You have no right here, I have the name of Jesus." Praise God, if you do that, he will back off.

That name has authority, but it will only benefit you when you use it. That's why Jesus said, "Whatever you bind on earth is bound in heaven; whatever you loose on earth is loosed in heaven" (Matthew 16:19; Matthew 18:18). When God sees you do it on earth, He sees Jesus doing it in heaven. When He sees you binding, Jesus is binding in heaven. When He sees you setting people free and loosing them, He sees them loosed in heaven.

You have that power. You have that right. You have that authority. Learn how to use it and go out and conquer, instead of being conquered.

Jesus said, *"Go ye therefore, and teach all nations, baptizing them in the name of the Father, and of the Son, and of the Holy Ghost"* (Matthew 28:19).

Some people are so **hung-up** on this business about "you have to be baptized in Jesus' name." Some say, "If you're not baptized in the name of the Father, the Son, and the Holy Ghost, you're not baptized."

One night on the telephone, a lady kept talking, on and on and on. She was telling me that I had to be baptized again, because I hadn't been baptized in Jesus' name.

I want to show you this. The above scripture that we just read says, "baptizing them in the name (n-a-m-e, singular)." Notice, it didn't say, "in the names of the Father, and of the Son, and the Holy Ghost. It said, "in **the name** of . . . ."

On earth, **the name** of the Father, the Son, and the Holy Ghost **is JESUS!** It doesn't matter whether you are baptized in the name of the Father, the Son and the Holy Ghost, or in the name of Jesus, you're still baptized, and God still accepts it.

When you hear the term, "the Father, the Son, and the Holy Ghost," it is talking about God the Father, about Jesus Christ, about the Holy Spirit. You know who that is, don't you?

So, it doesn't matter whether you are baptized in the name of the Father, the Son, and the Holy Ghost, or in the name of Jesus.

Personally I like to use the name of Jesus. I baptize in the name of Jesus because the book of Acts shows the early church doing it that way. But, I am not going to tell anybody that because they weren't baptized in Jesus' name that they aren't baptized. I was baptized in the name of the Father, the Son, and the Holy Ghost, and I defy any man to tell me I wasn't baptized. The Father accepted it, and that's what counts.

Praise God for the name of Jesus! *"Wherefore God also hath highly exalted him, and given him a name which is above every name: That at the name of Jesus every knee should bow, of things in heaven, and things in earth, and things under the earth; And that every tongue should confess that Jesus Christ is Lord, to the glory of God the Father"* (Philippians 2:9-11).

That means that Jesus' name has authority in the three worlds. "And that every tongue should confess that Jesus Christ is Lord, to the glory of God the Father." That day is coming, friend, but you can start confessing Him now. You can receive Christ as your Savior and begin to confess Him now, on your own terms, or you can wait until the angels put their feet on your neck and make you confess that Jesus is Lord to the glory of God, because that's what's going to happen.

The above passage also said, "Every knee should bow and every tongue should confess it." Now, you either do it willingly or unwillingly, but you are going to do it whether you like it or not.

Jesus Snatched The Keys—

That name has authority in the heavens. It has authority in earth. It has authority under the earth.

What do I mean, "under the earth"?

In the heart of the earth where the departed spirits of the wicked dead go, down to what is called "hades."

Jesus went down there and used that name and snatched the keys from Satan (the keys to the gates of hades). He said, "All power in heaven and earth is in my hand." He said, "I have the keys!"

That name is above every name. *"God, who at sundry times and in divers* (different) *manners spake in time past unto the fathers by the prophets* (That's in the Old Testament dispensation, the prophets Isaiah, Jeremiah, Amos, and all of those men), *Hath in these last days spoken unto us by his Son, whom he hath appointed heir of all things, by whom also he made the worlds; Who being the brightness of his glory, and the express image of his person, and upholding all things by the word of his power, when he had by himself purged our sins, Sat down on the right hand of the Majesty on high; Being made so much better than the angels, as he hath by inheritance obtained a more excellent name than they"* (Hebrews 1:1-4).

Glory to God! That more excellent name is at your disposal. That name has authority over all the powers of Satan, darkness, demons, poverty, sickness, degradation, anything negative that you can name.

We read earlier about the healing of the lame man, lame from his mother's womb. We saw how Peter used the authority of the name of Jesus.

In Acts 3:14-16, Peter and John had been brought before the Sanhedrin Council. That was equivalent to our Supreme Court. They were the highest ecclesiastical body in Judaism. They had the authority to hand down all the edicts about what the interpretation. of the Law was supposed to be. Peter and John were brought before them because they had healed this man. They will bring you in today if you perform too many miracles.

Peter, in giving his defense, said this: *"But ye denied the Holy One and the Just, and desired a murderer to be granted unto you* (Barabbas), *And killed the Prince of life, whom God hath raised from the dead; whereof we are witnesses. And his name through faith in his name hath made this man strong, whom ye see and know: yea, the faith which is by him hath given him this perfect soundness in the presence of you all."*

Peter said it was faith in the name of Jesus that made the man whole. Peter didn't say, "It's by my power." He didn't say, "It's by my authority." He didn't say, "It's because I have been with Jesus three and a half years." He didn't say, "It was because I knew something that nobody else knew." He said, "IT'S FAITH IN THE NAME OF JESUS."

If you don't have faith in the name, it won't work for you. Many of you say, "the name of Jesus," but you don't really believe in the name of Jesus. You just utter it intellectually. You say, "Jesus," but it doesn't mean anything to you.

Peter said, "It's faith in that name." Peter took that faith and used that name, and the man was healed!

In Acts 4:9-10, Peter is still talking, *"If we this day be examined of the good done to the impotent man, by what means he is made whole; Be it known unto you all, and to all the people of Israel, that by the name of Jesus Christ of Nazareth, whom ye crucified, whom God raised from the dead, even by him doth this man stand here before you whole."*

Thank God, the name of Jesus will make men whole in their spirits, in their souls, and in their bodies.

Let's look at another way that this name was used. *"And it came to pass, as we went to prayer, a certain damsel possessed with a spirit of divination met us, which brought her masters much gain by soothsaying* (telling the future): *The same followed Paul and us, and cried, saying, These men are the servants of the most high God, which show unto us the way of salvation. And this did she many days. But Paul, being grieved, turned and said to the spirit, I command thee in the name of Jesus Christ to come out of her. And he came out the same hour"* (Acts 16:16-18).

You Must Have The Authority Before You Use The Name Of Jesus—

Even the spirits know the authority that's in the name of Jesus. If you have not been born again, you better be very careful about what you do with the name of Jesus, because you can get yourself into a whole lot of trouble.

I'll show you what will happen to you if you fool around with the name of Jesus. If you are not a Christian, you don't have the authority to use it.

"Then certain of the vagabond Jews, exorcists, took upon them to call over them which had evil spirits the name of the Lord Jesus, saying, We adjure you by Jesus whom Paul preacheth.

"And there were seven sons of one Sceva, a Jew, and chief of the priests, which did so.

"And the evil spirit answered and said, Jesus I know, and Paul I know; but who are ye?

"And the man in whom the evil spirit was leaped on them, and overcame them, and prevailed against them, so that they fled out of that house naked and wounded" (Acts 19:13-16).

One man who has an evil spirit in him overcame seven grown men, and whipped their heads and sent them running, because they didn't have the right or the authority to use that name. They heard Paul do it and they said, "We are going to call this demon out of this man. We know this old guy that lives down on the other side of the tracks, we are going down there today and cast that demon out of him. We have a new method."

They ran in and said, "All right, in the name of Jesus, whom Paul preacheth, come out of that man."

That spirit took over the vocal apparatus of that man and said, "Paul, I know, Jesus I know, but (checked his list) I don't see your name on the list." He began whipping their heads.

They didn't have the authority to use the name of Jesus.

Praise God for the name of Jesus! That name that is above every name, the fairest of ten thousand, the lily of the valley, the bright and the morning star, the name of Jesus.

In the Old Testament Jacob prophesying over his children said, "The scepter shall not depart from Judah, nor a lawgiver from between his feet, until Shiloh come" (Genesis 49:10).

Thank God, 1900 years ago Shiloh came and when He went to that cross He handed to the Church the authority to use His name. Shiloh's already been here, friend. We have the use of His name. You talk about a *MASTER CARD*, a *VISA*, *AMERICAN EXPRESS*, all of those other cards. We have all of it together in the NAME OF JESUS! It will supply all your needs, and it will defeat every adversary.

When Jesus was getting ready to go back to heaven, He said, "**And these signs shall follow them that believe; in my name** (There's the name again) **shall they** (They who? They that believe) **cast out devils; they shall speak with new tongues** (languages); **They shall take up serpents; and if they drink any deadly thing, it shall not hurt them; they shall lay hands on the sick, and they shall recover**" (Mark 16:17-18).

How are we going to do those things?

We are going to do them **in the name of Jesus.**

Do you know that name? Do you know the authority that's in that name? Have you used that authority?

If you haven't, you are living below your privileges. If you are a born-again Christian, if you know Jesus Christ as your personal Savior, you have the right to use that NAME!

You can sit there in your pride and your religious tradition, and you can be buffeted about by the enemy. You can be poor, and you can be blind; you can be naked and you can be defeated. But don't blame God. Don't try to put it under the **guise** that you are suffering for the Lord, to bring glory to Him, because you are lying.

He has given YOU the authority of that NAME to break the power of Satan over your life.

Praise God! Principle number six: **You must Know the Reality of the Authority of the Name of Jesus.**

If you will master and apply these six principles that I have given you, you will most definitely be the possessor of strong faith. I use these principles in every area of my life and my faith has soared as a result of it.

How To Obtain Strong Faith — Six Principles: Use them; and instead of being conquered, you will be more than a conqueror!

Words
of
Faith

So then faith cometh by hearing, and hearing by the word of God.

Romans 10:17

For ever, O Lord, thy word is settled in heaven.

Psalm 119:89

So shall my word be that goeth forth out of my mouth: it shall not return unto me void, but it shall accomplish that which I please, and it shall prosper in the thing whereto I sent it.

Isaiah 55:11

Then said the Lord unto me, Thou hast well seen: for I will hasten my word to perform it.

Jeremiah 1:12

I will worship toward thy holy temple, and praise thy name for thy lovingkindness and for thy truth: for thou hast magnified thy word above all thy name.

Psalm 138:2

But without faith it is impossible to please him: for he that cometh to God must believe that he is, and that he is a rewarder of them that diligently seek him.

Hebrews 11:6

For by grace are ye saved through faith; and that not of yourselves: it is the gift of God: not of works, lest any man should boast.

Ephesians 2:8,9

And Jesus answering saith unto them, Have faith in God. For verily I say unto you, that whosoever shall say unto this mountain, Be thou removed, and be thou cast into the sea; and shall not doubt in his heart, but shall believe that those things which he saith shall come to pass; he shall have whatsoever he saith. Therefore I say unto you, What things soever ye desire, when ye pray, believe that ye receive them, and ye shall have them.

Mark 11:22-24

Therefore being justified by faith, we have peace with God through our Lord Jesus Christ: by whom also we have access by faith into his grace wherein we stand, and rejoice in hope of the glory of God.

Romans 5:1,2

For though I be absent in the flesh, yet am I with you in the spirit, joying and beholding your order, and the stedfastness of your faith in Christ. As ye have therefore received Christ Jesus the Lord, so walk ye in him: rooted and built up in him, and stablished in the faith, as ye have been taught, abounding therein with thanksgiving.

Colossians 2:5-7

Let us draw near with a true heart in full assurance of faith, having our hearts sprinkled from an evil conscience, and our bodies washed with pure water. Let us hold fast the profession of our faith without wavering; (for he is faithful that promised;) Now the just shall live by faith: but if any man draw back, my soul shall have no pleasure in him.

Hebrews 10:22,23,38

Looking unto Jesus the author and finisher of our faith; who for the joy that was set before him endured the cross, despising the shame, and is set down at the right hand of the throne of God.

For consider him that endured such contradiction of sinners against himself, lest ye be wearied and faint in your minds. Ye have not yet resisted unto blood, striving against sin.

Hebrews 12:2-4

Knowing this, that the trying of your faith worketh patience.

James 1:3

But ye, beloved, building up yourselves on your most holy faith, praying in the Holy Ghost, keep yourselves in the love of God, looking for the mercy of our Lord Jesus Christ unto eternal life.

Jude 20,21

And being not weak in faith, he (Abraham) considered not his own body now dead, when he was about an hundred years old, neither yet the deadness of Sarah's womb:

He staggered not at the promise of God through unbelif; but was strong in faith, giving glory to God; and being fully persuaded that, what he had promised, he was able also to perform.

Romans 4:19-21

Above all, taking the shield of faith, wherewith ye shall be able to quench all the fiery darts of the wicked.

Ephesians 6:16

About the Author

Dr. Frederick K.C. Price is the founder and pastor of Crenshaw Christian Center in Los Angeles, California. He is known worldwide as a teacher of the biblical principles of faith, healing, prosperity and the Holy Spirit. During his more than 47 years in ministry, countless lives have been changed by his dynamic and insightful teachings that truly "tell it like it is."

His television program, *Ever Increasing Faith*, has been broadcast throughout the world for more than 20 years and airs in 15 of the 20 largest markets in America, reaching an audience of more than 15 million households each week. His radio program is heard on stations across the world, including the continent of Europe via short-wave radio. He is the author of more than 50 popular books teaching practical application of biblical principles.

Dr. Price pastors one of America's largest church congregations, with a membership of 20 thousand. The church sanctuary, the FaithDome, is among the most notable and largest in the nation, with seating capacity of more than 10 thousand.

In 1990, Dr. Price founded the Fellowship of Inner City Word of Faith Ministries (FICWFM). Members of FICWFM include more than 300 churches from all over the United States and various countries. The Fellowship, which meets regionally throughout the year and hosts an annual convention, is not a denomination. Its mission is to provide fellowship, leadership, guidance and a spiritual covering for those desiring a standard of excellence in ministry. Members share methods and experiences commonly faced by ministries in the inner cities. Their focus is how to apply the Word of Faith to solve their challenges.

Dr. Price holds an honorary Doctorate of Divinity degree from Oral Roberts University and an honorary diploma from Rhema Bible Training Center.

On September 6, 2000, Dr. Price was the first black pastor to speak at Town Hall Los Angeles. In 1998, he was the recipient of two prestigious awards: The Horatio Alger Award, which is given each year. This prestigious honor is bestowed upon ten "outstanding Americans who exemplify inspirational success, triumph over adversity, and an uncommon commitment to helping others ...." He also received the 1998 Southern Christian Leadership Conference's Kelly Miller Smith Interfaith Award. This award is given to clergy who have made the most significant contribution through religious expression affecting the nation and the world.

To receive Dr. Price's book and tape catalog
or be placed on the EIF mailing list,
please call:

(800) 927-3436

*Books are also available
at local bookstores everywhere.*

For more information, please write:

**Crenshaw Christian Center
P.O. Box 90000
Los Angeles, CA 90009**

or check your local TV listing:

**Ever Increasing Faith
Television Program**

or visit our Websites:

**www.faithdome.org
www.faithdome.tv**